NEVERTHELESS . . .

"'Something has to be done about this' is a cry that rose in the heart of a young teenager, when arriving on the scene to see an arrogant, God-hating, giant defying, what should have been a confident covenant minded army. As he was breathing an atmosphere of negativity, fear and cowardice, it was that cry that caused David to become a hero in a day. Every great leader that has left their mark in history started here.

"John Kirkby's story is the result of a man who looked at the Goliath of debt, robbing people of dignity, property and security and cried, 'something needs to be done about this' it's an amazing, inspiring true story of what God can do in a human heart with that cry."

Ray Bevan
Senior Pastor
The King's Church
Newport South Wales

"John Kirkby is one of those people who has decided not to leave this world the same way he found it. Despite personal setback and heartfelt pain, he is a shining example of the things that God can do for a man, in a man and through a man when he is totally dedicated to serve the Lord. This practical journal will give information and encouragement for others who also believe that they are here to make a difference. Without doubt it will make us all realise we only have one life, so let's make it a life worth living."

Andrew Owen
Senior Pastor
Destiny Church Glasgow
Founder of Destiny Ministries

"If you like a good human story, you'll love this! It is the story of one life, but, more importantly in many ways, the potential that one life had to influence so many more. What makes it remarkable is the relatively short period it covers. John was saved only eleven years ago and CAP is only seven years old! If God can do so much through one life dedicated to his purpose in those few years, what can he do through a lifetime? John's story will inspire you to get in touch with that which God wants you to do for him in your lifetime and get on with it. Who knows what you will encounter along the way? Only God, and as you tenaciously hold onto His promise, one day you too will say 'Nevertheless' God's word is sure!"

Stephen Matthew
Associate Pastor
Abundant Life Church, Bradford.

Nevertheless . . .

*The incredible story of
one man's mission to change
thousands of people's lives*

JOHN KIRKBY
with Marianne Clough

CHRISTIANS AGAINST POVERTY BOOKS
Bradford

First published 2003
Reprinted 2005

Published by Christians Against Poverty Books,
Jubilee Mill, North Street, Bradford, BD1 4EW

ISBN 0 9546410 0 0

Biblical quotations are taken from
NIV – the New International Version © 1973,
1978, 1984 by the International Bible Society; and from
RSV – Revised Standard Version copyrighted 1946, 1952, © 1971,
1973 by the Division of Christian Education and Ministry of the
National Council of the Churches of Christ in the USA.

Printed in Great Britain.
Book design and production for the publisher by
Bookprint Creative Services, P.O. Box 827, BN21 3YJ, England.

CONTENTS

INTRODUCTION

Welcome to the story of how God transformed my life, how Christians Against Poverty was born and how it has grown. As it unfolds you will read of my early life, how I became a Christian, and a history of the events, people and struggles covering the first seven years of our work.

I am grateful for the individuals who gave me permission to include their names and those who have been brave enough to let me use their testimonies. Obviously, this is how I have seen things. It's my personal perception of events, and others may have seen them differently. Some of the diary accounts were written in the midst of some difficult and amazing times and are a little raw in places. My intention is to simply give you a true feel for what was going on.

I want to say a very special thank you to Marianne Clough who has worked with me tirelessly over the last six months to take my raw book and transform it into this finished work. Marianne is a talented Christian journalist who worked for the Bradford Telegraph and Argus back in 1997 when she wrote the first newspaper article about our work. She has always been a great supporter and encourager of both CAP and myself. It was her insistence that, as she put it "we only have one chance to tell this story right" that inspired me to keep going over the last six months.

This book is dedicated to my wonderful, supportive and loving wife Lizzie who has stuck with me through thick and thin, to my four children Jasmine, Jessica, Abigail and Thomas and our new baby due in February 2004! Also to my ever faithful mum, and to my pastor for 11 years and the man who brought me to the Lord, Paul Hubbard. It is also dedicated to my great friends and co-workers Matt and Josie Barlow, who have been by my side through the last challenging four and a half years and to all CAP staff and supporters past and present. Without their combined belief in and support of the vision God placed in me, this story could not have been told.

Finally and most importantly I dedicate this book to my Lord and Saviour Jesus Christ. Without His wonderful faithful presence, guidance, wisdom and encouragement there simply would be nothing to write about.

My prayer is that your faith in the Lord is increased and that your understanding of how He can work is broadened. I pray also that you will sense the awesome deeds He can perform through normal men and women just like you and me.

To Him be all the glory, honour and praise.

CHAPTER ONE

JOHN KIRKBY

The Early Years

As a family we were members of the United Reformed Church in the West Yorkshire woollen town of Heckmondwike where I was born on October 25, 1961. My mum who has a great faith, took me every Sunday. I knew about God but had no real understanding of who He really was.

My sisters Susan and Judith were 12 and 13 years older than me and had both flown the nest by the time I was seven, so I enjoyed the attention of both my parents as if I had been an only child.

My dad was from a fairly poor background but had worked his way up through a seven-year apprenticeship to be an electrician, and then over 15 years to become an electrical engineer for the BBA Group in nearby Cleckheaton. The firm made brake linings and conveyor belts. A handsome man with half-rimmed glasses, my dad was forever tinkering with electronics and he actually invented several things that had successful patents. One was a gadget to stop people cutting their hands on a machinery blade. If you had ventured into the loft of our otherwise ordinary three-bed semi, you would have found it filled with the most impressive model railway that my dad had built and completely automated. He would come down for tea leaving six tracks worth of trains eerily stopping and starting by themselves without ever bumping into each other.

In my early life I was his constant companion. I was the son he had always wanted and as I arrived later on in his life he had a lot of time to dote on me. He was willing to go fishing, exploring, and I have lovely memories of us damming rivers and that kind of thing. His loving and gentle nature was a great influence on my early life. My mum cared enormously for me and tried hard to keep me on the straight and narrow. She was always kind and generous and very forgiving, which was a good thing. I have so much to thank them for, not least the loving environment they brought me up in. I was really blessed and it left me feeling very, very secure.

Aged 3: damming a river, Scotland 1964

My Mum looked after me while, for the last nine years of his life, my father had long spells in hospital. They gave me a healthy self-esteem and encouraged me in whatever I undertook. Great parents are of huge value.

I was bright at school despite mild dyslexia. But I was really top of the tree in the playground. I was confident and popular and I was one of those who picked the games we played. I lost my front tooth in the process of holding my own, so as you see the fighting spirit was alive in me from the start.

To my great regret I left the church at age 11 as soon as my mum finally said I could. However, I had a definite awakening of my faith when I was 14 during a showing of the film "The Cross and the Switchblade". It told the true story of how a Christian pastor took on a dead inner-city church surrounded by gangs and drugs and made it work for the Lord.

After the film I remember standing in front of my mates with tears running down my face. I went forward and spent some time with a young lad who explained it was Jesus, and I think I prayed the prayer of salvation. My mum's church minister tried his best to get hold of me, and I went to at least one bible group and a young peoples' group twice. After that, the pull of the world and my mates just drew me back.

Only God knows what would have happened to me had I continued then with the faith God had obviously stirred in me. I feel this particularly as I see my eldest daughters Jasmine, 17, and Jessica, 13, involved in a great youth group. They have their own faith, going away with friends for events like "Soul Survivor". Even though I gave up on God, He never gave up on me.

When I was just nine, my father – a teetotaller – contracted a virus that led to a serious liver illness that brought about his death nine years later when he was just 57. My father was very ill for the majority of my teenage years, and I have to say I was by no means a perfect son. I was quite rebellious, with a gift for getting into trouble; I steadily progressed through all the vices. He was in hospital for long periods of time, and I would visit whenever I could. I now know that the true extent of his illness was kept from me until near his death. One of my greatest regrets is that in the years running up to his death he may have seen me as a rebellious, ungrateful, self-ish teenager. I often wonder what he thought of his beloved son when he saw me making such a mess of my teenage years. I hope he saw through all that and believed I would come good one day.

I still miss him and can very easily be overcome emotionally with the loss. It's one of those things that, for me, doesn't get easier with the passing of time. With the birth of my fourth child Tommy (full name Thomas Donald after his grandad), my sense of loss has been increased. My dad was 40 when I was born, the same age I was when Tommy turned up. When I hold and play with Tommy, I have often thought of the love my dad must have had for me. How he must have loved me as I love my son. It is a hard thing to lose your father so early on.

Aged 1¹/₂: 1963 elections. Dad stood as prospective Liberal councillor

My working life begins

Heckmondwike Grammar School's headmaster was in shock at the six O Levels I achieved there. Certainly I hadn't shown a great deal of promise in the run-up to them. But the fighting spirit came through again for me, and I had crammed all the way to the finish. Not bad for someone who had almost "opted out" of school a year earlier.

At 15 I took extra time off school over the summer to work at a local paint factory where I lied about my age to get in. I made up a National Insurance number, so someone somewhere owes me some contributions! They took me on to be a "Lidder" (Yes, that's where you bang a lid on a paint tin with a wooden mallet!). After a couple of weeks I got promoted to a "Stacker" (Where you stack full tins of paint on a pallet!) and then within a few weeks I reached the highest level within the team, a "Filler" (I had to open and close a pipe with a lever to fill tins of paint). It may not have been the most impressive career start but a least I got the top job. However the job was the easy bit . . .

Working place directives had not reached Norman Driver Surface Coatings in the 1970s. Violence and bullying were endemic and I literally had to fight other lads to avoid being beaten. Had my mum and dad known this they would have got me out.

I hardened up very quickly and although I would never wish this type of experience on any young person it did make me realise this life was going to be a bit tougher than I had thought. If I was to get on I would need to use all my wits, work hard and wise up very quickly.

One job no one else in the factory wanted to do was to take the sandwich orders, but I remember jumping at the chance to get out for an hour or two. Within days I had negotiated with two sandwich firms, got them to knock their prices down and was pocketing the difference – entrepreneurial or what?! After eight weeks of this I returned to school to see out the last few months a little humbled by what the real world was like.

After my O Levels, I took a commercial apprenticeship with a local engineering company and for the next two years learned basic office systems and studied, somewhat unsuccessfully, for an ONC in business studies at Huddersfield College.

My father died quite suddenly on February 3, 1980. He had seemingly recovered many times only to lapse back into serious illness and this had become normal to us all. He was a real fighter who never complained but just fought and fought. I got used to the fact that he kept getting better. Well, one day he didn't and died peacefully in his sleep. I was the first to reach the hospital and I looked into his face and held his hand. Somehow he looked at rest. I think that after such a hard nine-year battle his body just said, "I have had enough".

It was a traumatic time for the whole family. My mum managed to be very strong for us all but within a year it became too much for her to bear and she became very ill and had to go into hospital for a time. This left me – age 19 – living at home on my own and visiting her in hospital while trying to progress in a new and very demanding job. All that great care-free time in your late teens I crammed into the weekends. Picture me, if you will, at this time. I had a bike and leathers and was into heavy music and all that goes with it, basically off the rails Friday to Sunday.

I met my first wife Anne, in a rock club in Dewsbury about two months after my dad's death. We married in 1982 after three years together. We were just 20 and 21. When we first got together she was doing teacher training in Scarborough. She was beautiful, relaxed and great fun. I would finish work on a Friday and race up to Scarborough with my mates to spend wild weekends sleeping in the back of vans roughing it and wonder at the student culture I was missing out on. Then it would be haring back home in the early hours of a Monday morning with enough time to change into my suit and tie ready for the ridiculously sensible day job.

Around the time of dad's death, I had what would turn out to be a decisive career change. I just got sick of boring office work and walked into the Brighouse job centre one dinnertime. I saw a job for an "Accounts Representative" with an American finance company called Avco Trust. I applied and got the job. It turned out that it was a posh name for a debt collector and loan salesman.

The company was very good at training and I learned a lot of the basic skills in managing people, businesses, dealing with the public and how the finance industry worked. They were not interested in academic achievement. They wanted to know if you would work hard and get results. They had competitions and were really success orientated and I thrived in that environment. Over the next two years I got stuck in and discovered what I was good at: communicating and dealing with people, working very hard and getting things done. I had a rapid rise within the company and at 21 became the manager of their Doncaster office, one of the youngest they had ever had. Over the next seven years I had a very successful career with Avco, running several branches, and I continued to prosper in both business and at home.

As I reflect on this time, it's obvious to me that I had no real idea of the misery some customers were going though. I was just trying hard to do my job. This has helped me over the years when dealing with and understanding how the whole finance industry works.

During this time, my first daughter Jasmine was born in September 1986. The birth of your first child must rank as one of the most amazing experiences of your life. To hold my own daughter in my hands was something I will never forget. Right from the word go she was so bright, sharp and quick to learn. She walked at seven months and you could have an adult conversation with her when she was just 18 months old. Jasmine has grown into a wonderful young woman of whom I am very proud.

My second daughter Jessica came along in 1990. She is so full of life, with a very gentle and loving nature. She is very bright like her eldest sister and very much full of grace and compassion for others. Jessica is growing up and making the most of her life.

By now I had left Avco and I worked for a year setting up and pioneering a new contract hire and leasing company in the motor trade. I was eventually appallingly treated by my boss and unceremoniously sacked. Determined never to work for anyone ever again, I started my own business – building, hiring and selling sun beds working from my garage. I had got the idea from one of the companies I had helped get vehicles for. I was staggered by the amount of money they were making. My sister Susan and brother-in-law Stewart joined me after a couple of years as we became the largest sunbed retailer in the north of England. I then began to expand into numerous, ultimately, less successful businesses. I grew my own small finance company which financed the sun bed sales, and I also started a financial services company and a loan brokerage company. I even experimented with building and selling houses. Last but by no means least I started an estate agency business.

As I look back on that time, I am overwhelmed by just how much of an entrepreneurial spirit God had given me. However, without wisdom and left unchecked, it would eventually result in my businesses collapsing. But I learned so much about turning ideas into reality. I had everything the world deems successful: a beautiful wife, two lovely children, six bed secluded house, cars, holidays and money in the bank. It was actually all built on sand with nothing underneath it, as I was soon to find out.

In early 1992 my whole world fell apart. I made many mistakes and had borrowed huge sums of money from banks to finance my business operations. Banks started to ask for their money back and a house I had built plummeted in value before I could sell it. I might have looked fine on the outside but inside I was a broken, lonely man watching all he had worked for being lost before his very eyes. I remember one day very vividly, it sums up what I went through and how bad it all got.

My accountant basically told me that I should go bankrupt as my interest payments and overheads were so huge and my assets had become almost worthless. Every day I had to manage several businesses and juggle huge sums of money just to get through. I used credit cards to pay wages and suppliers etc. It was a crazy time of ever increasing problems, pressure and difficulties. Something had to give. However there was one glimmer of hope and that was that we were very close to selling the estate agency for £30,000.

Things had looked very rosy when I started the estate agency, with a friend in the late 1980s but the collapse of the housing market just destroyed us. We had increasing debts of over £30,000, which we had borrowed to keep the business afloat and the lease on our shop had four years to run. The landlord was threatening to sue us for the whole four years' rent – over £25,000. However, we had agreed to sell the business for £30,000 to a company backed by Sun Alliance and this would have cleared our debts. They had also agreed to take over the lease we had on the premises. This would have given me half a chance, as the other businesses were relatively sound. The day before we were due to   complete I was informed that the deal was off, due to increased nervousness in the housing market.

There I was in my beloved 2.8i Granada Scorpio – personalised number plates, full body kit, cruising speed of 140mph, you get the picture. I switched off the mobile, started her up and began instinctively to drive home. A few hundred yards from home I simply pulled off the road into a pub car park and passed out with physical and emotional stress. Anne was driving six-year-old Jasmine home from school who spotted her daddy's car and they pulled over. I remember being awoken by Jasmine knocking on my car window saying: "Daddy, Daddy wake up". Anne took me home and I collapsed, almost went into a semi-coma for two days. I alone knew what this all meant for us as a family, and the pain was excruciating. As I sit and write this book some ten years later it still makes me shudder to remember how I felt. Virtually everything had been lost and I found myself with huge debts totalling over £78,000 and nowhere to turn.

Over the next week as I came round to the facts I somehow managed to pull myself together and something inside me said I will not go under without a fight. I began to do what I could to minimise the difficulties. I knew I was fighting a losing battle but nevertheless I carried on. I wasn't to know that just around the corner I was about to encounter the living God, my Saviour, in a most dramatic way.

CHAPTER TWO

THE LORD INTERVENES

I had a four-bedroomed detached house in Baildon, North Bradford, which I had ended up with thanks to a brave but fool-hardy property deal. It had a huge mortgage on it and I was desperate to sell it to reduce my interest payments and get rid of one more headache.

One Saturday I received a phone call from a bloke who said he was a pastor who had just come over from his wife's home coun-try, Norway. He and his young family had nowhere to live and he wanted to know if he could rent my house. This man was Pastor Paul Hubbard who was to become one of the most influential people in my life. I remember thinking: a pastor as a tenant is the last thing I need!

How wrong could I have been? Over a period of a few months I got to know Paul and his wife Kjersti. They invited me to their home and befriended me. Despite my problems, I became involved in their struggles. They had nothing when they arrived. I even bought them some carpets with some of the rent they paid as they had so little. However they seemed so at peace with life and so open and caring towards my family and me.

Then on Wednesday evening June 24, 1992 as I collected my

rent, Paul simply gave me a Bible and said they had been praying for me. He asked me: "Would you like to come to our church on Sunday?" I took the Bible and said: "Yes, I will."

As I walked in the door that night I felt different. Anne was the first to notice it as soon as I came in. She said: "What's happened to you?"

I went to the church the next week, July 5, 1992. It was a small church in Shipley, north of Bradford, called Charlestown Baptist. I just knew there was something there I was supposed to yield to. I now know this was the love of Jesus reaching out to one needy man. Paul asked me back for a coffee and I gave my life to the Lord in his kitchen. I was baptised in December 1992.

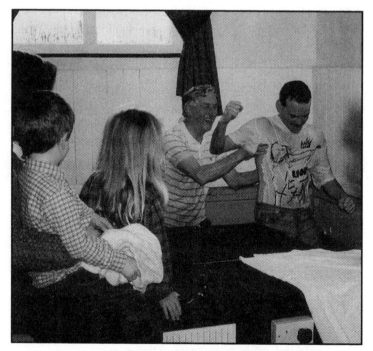

Being baptised by Derrick Clarke: 6th December 1992,
Charlestown Baptist Church

Who would have thought, when I put that house up for sale, God would come knocking on my door? I was instantly on fire for Him. Straight away I was visiting sick people in Bradford Royal Infirmary with a guy called Martin Jones. We just went onto wards and started talking to and praying for sick people we didn't even know. I also remember being on an outreach and stopping cars at a roundabout to give them tracts and talking to them about Jesus. (Zealot or what?!)

We moved with the majority of the congregation, to start Christian Life Church Shipley, in February 1996. It was in this church that CAP was born a few months later.

At this point I know that I'm supposed to say my life went from strength to strength but the truth is somewhat different and I embarked on what was to become one of the most difficult two years of my life.

Although saved, I was still living in between the world and the Lord. I was really mixed up and did many things I regretted later. Whenever I hear of new or long-standing Christians having difficulties, I always think back to how far short I fell, and still fall, as a Christian. Perhaps that's how God gives us the grace and compassion we need for our brothers and sisters when they struggle.

My financial situation continued to worsen. It wasn't one aspect of the business that was going into melt-down, it was many, all at the same time and the unthinkable was being played out in front of me, regardless of the efforts I made.

This pressure and my past mistakes were to be the seeds of our eventual marriage breakdown, as we simply grew apart. However, to this day Anne and I remain good friends and have both worked hard to keep things amicable between us.

I used to look out of the window and see my girls playing in the garden knowing in my heart their parents' marriage was over and I'd lost them their home. I felt so guilty that I'd had so much and blown the lot. I felt incredible shame. My accountant said I needed to find £1,000 a week to meet the interest payments or face bankruptcy. The stresses took their toll on my marriage and in February 1994 Anne and I separated. I praise God for the positive relationship we have subsequently managed to maintain for the sake of our beautiful daughters.

Over the next year I gradually fell apart. I was a completely broken man, living in a shell, shattered and breaking up. I used to look after my two girls Jasmine, then aged seven, and Jessica, four, every alternate weekend from Friday to Sunday and one night a week. I lived with a friend called Stan Fox who looked after me and was very supportive. When the girls stayed we used two camp beds in my one small room. I would often cry just looking at them both asleep next to me. The word "destitute" is often over used but that's what I became: utterly devoid of any spirit, hurting, lonely and afraid. I now know that God used this and other desperate experiences in my life. It was through these traumatic times that a greater sense of His love, forgiveness and heart for me became more and more real. I also began to have an ever-increasing compassion for others who were in need.

If you have ever judged or been unsympathetic towards a single parent and judged them for struggling, try it yourself for just a couple of days. If you are a single parent my heart goes out to you and I pray you will be strengthened as you try so hard alone. God knows your struggles and He is there to help you.

If right now you are thinking: "I'm in no fit state to serve God and I will never get into a place where God can use me", be encouraged. Can you ever imagine anybody less likely to be able to start a Christian Ministry and see his past so dramatically used for God's glory as me? I remain to this day a man who can struggle and who has weaknesses and difficulties but still He uses me. There is no one beyond the love and hope that is in Jesus.

Over the next two years I resurrected my career in the consumer finance industry working for Welcome Financial Services, a company I helped start back in the late 1980s. I was running their secured lending department, which we started in Bradford. It grew very rapidly and was the first place I began to see the blessing of God in my life. If it wasn't for this job and the earning potential I now possessed, I know that the companies who I owed money to would have pushed me into bankruptcy. I still owed huge debts to various companies and I had to contact all my creditors and made arrangements to pay reduced repayments. Most were helpful. However, I needed everything I could muster to get some of them to stop taking me to court. A court order would have meant me losing my job and they knew it and used it against me. I would never have thought in those dark days that God was even then preparing me for what was to come. I was actually doing for myself what CAP was about to do for other people and I had no idea.

I can now see that my work was indeed blessed by God and we became one of the most profitable departments within the company. Due to a very generous profit share and fantastic salary I was able to rapidly reduce my debts, which had reached about £78,000 in 1992 down to £25,000 at the beginning of 1996. Praise the Lord for His provision.

The business of helping people to borrow money was making me feel more and more uneasy. I often dealt with people unable to pay back what they had borrowed and who were really struggling. My Christian heart was telling me to help them and I did what I could for them by reducing interest and accepting reduced payments. However, I had to be responsible to my employers and remain professional.

It was during this time that I started to get myself more and more sorted out with God in terms of getting my life in line with His word. I began to put the teaching I was getting into practice in my life. It took me about two years from being saved to get my head around the whole area of tithing and giving. I eventually understood that God provided me with all my income and let me keep up to 90%.

We often expect new Christians to get themselves sorted out immediately, to get a huge revelation from the moment they receive Christ. If that happens, then praise God! However, most people need time to allow God to renew their minds. We then get His revelation through His grace and patience. How come we often expect everyone else to get a revelation in a few minutes, when it has taken us years to get it? Let's get real. It takes most people time and grace to get things firmly established within them.

I am often reminded, very gently and graciously by the Lord, that I have just scratched the surface of His understanding and that there is plenty more for me to learn. No doubt I will get it wrong again in the future.

In March 1995, a strange and wonderful thing happened. Paul and Kjersti Hubbard were in their car in a car park at the Bradford Christian School, when they saw a young woman walking from the pre-school where she worked. They both looked at each other and said: "There's John's future wife". They were very sensible and arranged for us to meet with a few friends for a pizza and see what happened. Lizzie had no idea that Paul and Kjersti were orchestrating the event so we could meet. The first thing I noticed about Lizzie was her face, so bright and joyful. She wore a long denim dress with a little flower patch on it and she was constantly followed by the small group of children who were there. I was captivated and I invited her to my house for a barbecue. She had something very special about her. It shone out of her.

Lizzie brought me alive. I was completely besotted with her and her gentle spirit of love towards me. She accepted me like no one else. She was six years younger than me and single. She had become a committed Christian seven years earlier. She has said, in jest I hope, that she was waiting for "a knight in shining armour to sweep her off her feet" and got "an old bloke on a donkey, with emotional baggage and two children in tow". Lizzie was and remains unbelievably good with my two daughters, Jasmine and Jessica. She took us all on right from the first meeting. Her kindness to us all stands as a testimony of the grace and love God has poured into her and her willingness to serve and love others first.

We fell in love and grew together through the difficulties. In February 1996 we got engaged and a month later I left my job and started to prepare for the launch of CAP. Just to put the record straight, Lizzie did know that I was about to give up my career and start in full time ministry before we got married. She never hesitated and although I'm sure neither of us knew what we were to be asked to go through by the Lord we were certain God had brought us together. We were married at Church on the Way, Bradford, on July 27, 1996 – a truly wonderful day. When we returned from our honeymoon and a holiday with the girls on August 21, the work of Christians Against Poverty began in earnest.

I asked Paul Hubbard to give his impressions of what he has experienced with us through these times. Paul was the man who brought me to the Lord and who has been by my side over the last

11 years throughout my entire walk with God and the whole CAP story.

Paul writes . . .

When I first met John, he did not know the Lord and had no knowledge of His ways, workings or wonders. For some inexplicable reason (at least to John), he not only rented his house to us, he also partly furnished it, which was a miracle, since we had just arrived from Norway, with no home, no money and very few personal possessions.

We settled in and over the next few months were able to spend time with him; gently opening him up to the good news of what Jesus had done for him. It was not long before he had given over his life to the goodness and mercy of God and his life began to be dramatically effected. It is true to say that although those early years were painful, perhaps even traumatic, they were also blessed.

Here was a man who had been steeped in the ways of the world, had been caught up in the 'rat race' and perhaps viewed by many as successful. There is no doubt that God had given John a mega-sized gift. But as he came to know the power of God at work in his life, he was faced with himself, his life, his motives and the environment of God's Word, love and compassion, the journey of transformation began to take place.

I have of course many memories of that journey thus far, both of John and of what has become a wonderful life-transforming ministry and charity.

One of my most treasured memories is early on in the beginning of the ministry, when perhaps only the two of us were around. John had gone to court on behalf of and with a client; it was a particularly difficult and distressing situation. He had done everything he could, he had used all the God–given ability and gifting to save this couple from losing their home. I had remained at John's house in prayer. When John arrived I knew it had been painful and upsetting. He had no words to communicate what was going on in his heart or express the grief and depth of compassion he felt. We wept, it was all we could do.

It was at this moment I felt the love, compassion and goodness of God being born into the ministry. This is still very evident today in greater measure, a stream that flows, a foundation to build upon. The above situation has been replayed in different ways many times over in the last seven years.

My own tribute to John and to the Lord – who has so marvellously created, loved and developed him and continues to do so – is that he is a man of compassion, vision, passion and evangelism. The message about Jesus has become a living reality, which he not only hears, but hears with faith. This faith leads him to action, even in the midst of personal circumstances which in many other lives would disable and hinder.

For John, Christianity is a reality; full of possibilities and adventure.

May it be that for you too!

Paul Hubbard
Pastor Christian Life Church Bradford
Trustee Christians Against Poverty 1996-2003

CHAPTER THREE

CHRISTIANS AGAINST POVERTY IS BORN!

It was all starting to look very good on the outside again by 1996; a large beautiful home, soon to be married and a potentially lucrative financial future. I was due to become debt free within a couple of years, felt well-respected and growing with God all the time. However, I began to sense that I had a major decision to make. Either I continued to do it my way and really push for more 'success' or I put myself properly in God's hands and see where He would take me.

I had only been a Christian for four years and for the first two I really struggled. When I look back it's amazing to see that despite my enormous shortfall as a young Christian and my lack of understanding, God moved very quickly when I decided to live the life He wanted. If you have been lukewarm for God for some time, don't be surprised how quickly God moves when you put Him first.

Be encouraged if you have had difficulties and been away from God in a wilderness either brought on by circumstances or your own mistakes or any combination of the two, God is just a prayer and a decision away. He's ready, willing and able to restore all you might have lost.

In early March 1996, as I pondered these thoughts I realised that a window of opportunity was beginning to open. Within one year the department I was responsible for would begin to see a down turn in business and profits due to market changes. I didn't know what to do but it occurred to me this was a way to step out in faith and see if now was the time for God to begin to release me. It was my first tentative step of faith. The truth is, I might not have taken this step had I known what the next few years were about to bring. Praise God for His wisdom in shielding me from this.

Feeling God was in control, on March 9, 1996, I rang my Managing Director, Ian Cummine, and told him we should consider shutting the department that I had built up. I explained that within a year the whole mortgage market would change and we would lose the commercial advantage we had enjoyed for four years.

Ian Cummine had been very influential in my career to that date. He was the first to really believe in me and he was always very generous in salaries and bonuses throughout my time working for him, which was about ten years in total in two stretches. He was a very sharp businessman and understood exactly what I was saying. He listened and said: "Okay, we'll shut it then." Only 21 days later, I was made redundant. The department closed and business transferred. If I had wanted to stay on he would have found a place for me, I'm sure. I did all this a few weeks before my annual bonus was due. Ian was very generous. He paid my yearly bonus, something he didn't have to do. Again God's favour is with the ones who will put their faith in Him on the line. Looking back, I realised that God really honoured my integrity. With this pay out, I was able to cover the costs of our forthcoming wedding and put the next year's maintenance on one side for my children.

Ian actually came to see me at CAP in October 2002 and I was able to thank him personally for how he had helped me at that very difficult time in my life and for the very gracious and generous way he released me from working for him. He was stunned at what he saw and was very encouraging. When Ian was with me I really felt the Lord prompt me to witness to him and you just never know, maybe he will one day read the book, get the message and make the sharpest decision he has ever made.

Encouraged by my first act of faith, I decided to take another step. I began to look at starting a Christian building society, finance company or bank. These sound like outrageous ideas, but with my background and experience they weren't totally unrealistic.

Then God broke in when I took a couple of days away with Paul to attend a conference at Pilgrim Hall in East Sussex. It was a gathering of church leaders for teaching, rest and reflection. One morning I found myself in a queue for breakfast, which went into two rooms, I chose one. Then I randomly sat at one of eight tables and found myself next to a man I had never seen before or since. I shared my ideas, (how daft must they have sounded?). He said to ring Nigel De Rivar, who was a venture capitalist who might be able to help me start either a bank or a building society. Out of the blue, God miraculously led me to the next phone call that was to prove one of the most important of my life.

On June 6, 1996, I rang him. I found out he was neither a venture capitalist nor able to help with my request. Nevertheless, he did ask one of the most important questions anyone has ever asked me. He said: "Why don't you see what you can do without needing anyone to help you start or any huge sum of money. What could you do on your own *now*?"

I went straight to my computer, I can't remember even praying. I just typed *debt counselling* and a few other ideas. This was it! I knew this was it. I could start now and get stuck in. I had found something I was qualified and able to do. I did not have to wait for anything.

Over the next six weeks leading up to our marriage I spent loads of time seeking God's heart for the poor, praying and studying the Bible. I designed a brochure, looked into money advice and just pressed ahead. We had nothing but debts and no real idea what to do next. God obviously had put some entrepreneurial DNA within me that just said why not me? Why not now? I registered the charity and was surprised no one else had registered the name Christians Against Poverty.

Lizzie and I got married on July 27, 1996, a most wonderful day and an example of God's grace in my life. Here I was with a beautiful Christian bride who loved me and wanted to be with me for the rest of her life in whatever we would face. We were in a church with over a hundred of our friends, being married by Paul Hubbard, the man who had brought me to Christ and us together. Our God is truly awesome.

Less than a month after the big day, there was another! On August 22, 1996, Christians Against Poverty began.

I still can't believe that Lizzie was up for what we actually did. There she was as a new bride starting out life together and what did we do but get rid of all our security and start a Christian ministry with no money. I am eternally grateful for her, her faith in God and me and for letting me just get on with what the Lord had called me to do. To this day she has never asked me to lay the work down or complained when things get tough.

All ready to go, armed with our first £10 gift, faith that God was with us, a vision and a prayer, we started. I posted off the brochure to 80 Bradford Churches and everyone I knew, asking more than 400 people to support me. Then I simply sat back and waited for the cash and encouragement to flood in.

CHAPTER FOUR

CAP's FIRST CLIENTS

Shock one: *"This ministry thing can be hard"*. We had this naive idea that everybody who heard of our vision, including the wider church, would be falling over themselves to support and encourage us in our step of faith. We felt sure they would rally to our vision and our needs. In fact, over the first six months only about 15 people supported our work.

Then came shock number two: *"People who don't even know you will support you."* A lady called Janet who worked as a cashier at Lloyds bank noticed CAP's name on the paying-in book and asked for details of the work I was starting. This was the first time she had met me and to my utter amazement sent £500 the next day. This kept us going for another month, what an encouragement! Then we received an anonymous gift of £500, to this day I do not know who sent it. Two weeks later, Church on the Way, Bradford, sent CAP £1000 as a gift from the church – astounding.

I wrote a simple brochure, sent it out to churches and gave it to friends. One of those friends, Angie Fox, suggested CAP to my first two clients. In September 1996, armed with a pad, calculator, enthusiasm and faith that God would help me, I went to see my first clients.

My first two clients were Dennis and Denise. They were an ordinary couple living in an ex-council house. Denise was a school assistant and Dennis an auto-electrician. As soon as I sat down with Denise, the reality of what I was about to face over the coming years hit me. I listened as Denise explained how she had fallen into a spiral of borrowing to pay off debts, ever increasing interest payments and charges. She had reached a stage of total financial collapse; owing £24,000 to about ten companies. She was facing court action, possible eviction and repossession of her house due to not paying their mortgage. If that wasn't enough, she then told me her husband had absolutely no idea about any of it.

I took a deep breath and thought: "I know what to do in principle. I have spent 17 years of my life preparing for this moment. I can do this". Firstly, I tried to reassure her I could help, that there was hope. The first thing I needed to do was explain things to her husband Dennis. She was distraught but agreed I should come back and tell him everything. I returned and with some fear and trepidation told Dennis the truth. I reiterated that although it looked impossible, I could get them out of the mess if they worked with me. He went into shock. Tears were streaming down his face. He didn't understand how they had got into this desperate situation. He just wanted to hear their home was safe. He wanted hope.

So, we started to work with them. The basic process remains the same to this day. It took me about three months and involved detailed negotiations with each creditor, getting them to accept reduced payments and to agree to stop charging any additional interest or add other charges. Dennis and Denise agreed not to borrow any more and to live within a budget. This meant that if they lived within their means, paid their disposable income to their creditors, through CAP, and did not borrow any more money, they would be debt free in five years. Their mortgage and other priority payments such as gas, electricity, council tax, including agreed arrears repayment, would be paid first. This would stop any repossession action by the mortgage company. They were so grateful for the release of the pressure and simply did what they had agreed to do. The results were amazing and over the last six years it has been my privilege to see their circumstances change out of all recognition.

Denise with John in May 2003 when she closed her account debt free, and moved into a new home

They saved up for years for their 25th wedding anniversary and went away for a cruise. It was such a joy when in May 2003 they were able to close their budget account. Totally debt free, in a new house and in charge of their money. That is what CAP's all about. It's about giving people a future hope and watching as their lives change before your eyes. Every month we see families come to the end of three, four and five year plans totally debt free and with their whole lives ahead of them. They are able to manage their finances; save and not borrow. Dennis and Denise will always be the first couple who trusted CAP's way and they are an inspiration and encouragement to us all and the thousands of families that have followed them over the years.

Dennis and Denise's situation was fairly shocking but the next three months, up to Christmas, were to fill me with compassion time and time again. I saw things that really opened my eyes: families with hungry children, people in trauma having no hope, broken marriages, and the sheer havoc and distress financial difficulties bring about in people's lives. Their strife had a profound effect on me. They were what inspired me to drive forward and see more people helped. It was strange that right from the first few weeks I knew I was born for this work and the thought of giving up never entered my mind. We had people who needed us. We simply had to carry on.

In the midst of all this, I was struggling with the way so many people responded so negatively to our work and vision. Christians berated me for, as they saw it, "my lack of responsibility for my own family's needs". Surely I should "Get a proper job and provide for my wife and children". Other people thought because we lived in a nice house, that I had some sort of "stash of cash". How wrong could they have been? We were living from week to week, our mortgage was more than the house was worth and was beginning to go unpaid, and we were struggling with the remainder of our debts. Collection companies were threatening us with court action. Some people just blanked us. We could not understand why people were not willing to encourage and support us.

One particular letter caused me much distress and pain.

Accusations were made against my personal integrity suggesting that my whole reason for starting CAP was for my own financial gain. I was accused of trying to make money out of the very people I was trying to help. All my efforts were utterly mocked and venomously attacked. Who did I think I was and what was I trying to achieve? Nothing I had done had amounted to much before so who was I trying to kid? Even my Christian faith was called into question and ridiculed.

I struggled with the tremendous sense of hurt and injustice at how I had been written off with such malice. Right when I was starting out, right when I was vulnerable, weak in faith and wondering what I had done, this rubbish had come through the letterbox.

This letter for the first time drew me to my old friend Nehemiah and in particular chapter six verse eight where he had just received an open letter accusing him of false proclamations. Nehemiah simply says: "Nothing like you are saying is happening; you are just making it up out of your head." Nehemiah's spirit said, I am not concerned with what you think. He just got on with it, he knew the truth and that God was with him.

After a few days of being very down-hearted I can remember realising I could do nothing to vindicate myself. God knew and it was His opinion I was interested in, not what other people thought. I now see that I was starting the process of being released from "what other people think" syndrome. This is a disabling spirit that makes you bound to the opinions of others, rather than what God thinks and what you know is right.

Over the next two years these problems persisted with accusations being levelled not just at me personally but questioning the integrity of the charity as a whole. They made accusations about our accounts, threatened to report us to the Charity Commission and even rang up demanding copies of our accounts. At one stage Paul Hubbard, by then the chairman of the charity, wrote to them asking them to come and see for themselves the value of our work and to allay their fears. They never took him up on the offer and eventually fell silent.

The whole area of people not supporting or encouraging us is a difficult one. With the benefit of a little wisdom and maturity, I now realise that of course not everyone is going to get behind and support your dream. Many people are pursuing and supporting other visions. I was naive to expect everybody to support me.

Another difficulty was and still is explaining our philosophy of employing people rather than waiting for volunteers. All along, CAP's main expense has been wages because we believe – and the Bible tells us – that a worker is worth his wage. It would be unrealistic to expect the full-time commitment of such professional people if we asked them to volunteer. Mortgages have to be paid and lives have to be lived. If they are willing to work hard for us, stand in faith and give so much, it is our responsibility as a charity to make sure those needs are met. That's why we are so committed to paying good salaries and benefits.

Still reeling from this hurtful letter, I met my second ever client. She came to me through a local vicar, the Rev Charles Barber, who I had met and sent some brochures to. He had a lady in his church in great distress. He gave her the CAP brochure and suggested I could be of help.

Her name was Debbie Thompson. She was to become perhaps the most influential client CAP has ever had. I want to give you her story from my perspective and then Debbie, in her own words, will explain how CAP affected her life and where the Lord has brought her today.

I remember the day I walked into Debbie's house. Her situation was as desperate as any I have seen. She was giving all her money to aggressive and manipulative collectors leaving her with virtually none with which to feed her children. She was within a few weeks of having her house repossessed, with spiralling debts. She would make just a few pounds feed her family for days. She would make dumplings from 9p bags of flour and just buy tins of beans or spaghetti to feed her two sons.

She told me how when working as an auxiliary nurse she would go to work with no food and just enough bus fare to get home because she had given all of her wage to satisfy debt collectors. She described how when the 'hat' went round for gifts for her work friends who were leaving or getting married she would have to go into the toilet to avoid the embarrassment of not having 50p to put in. She knew that people used to say, behind her back, that she was stingy. Yet Debbie is one of the most generous people you could ever meet.

Being in debt can be a private hell with no escape; it is an ever increasing torment and hardship. Debbie's case, together with another lady who was near to suicide when I went to see her, were the ones that really got me determined to make CAP grow and succeed. I became desperate to see thousands of other families released from such oppression and hopelessness into a future with God.

She was such a gentle lady, full of honour, yet broken and with no hope. I completed a financial statement and basically got stuck in with her creditors. I eventually got them to agree to reduced payments, stabilised the finances and Debbie and her family began to live a decent life.

Over the last six years, Debbie has become a legend and part of the very fabric of CAP. In 1998 she became a Trustee of the charity and to this day she remains on our management board and gives great wisdom and insight right into the heart of what we do. In 2000, she came with me to the Houses of Parliament to speak to the members and representatives of the finance industry about how poverty affects real people.

In 2001, Debbie volunteered to look after prayer for the charity. In October 2002, she assumed the employed position of National Prayer Co-ordinator. From near suicide in 1996, with the possibility of losing her home, to overseeing prayer for CAP – our God is truly an awesome God.

Debbie writes . . .

My first contact with John Kirkby was in September 1996. I telephoned him in tears, absolutely desperate. My husband and I had basically spiraled into debt over a period of six years. We had started well, having a thriving business, buying our own home and having two beautiful sons. Unfortunately the business dwindled and our attempts to sort it out only made things worse.

I was working nights nursing and we took on a second business. I was working myself to a standstill. I was deeply ashamed of being in debt and really wanted to fulfil our financial commitments but it became impossible. We were receiving constant telephone calls and letters pressuring us to make payments and I often felt so bad I just paid what they asked for and I would leave us with no money for food. I totally lost perspective of the situation. I would wake each morning just dreading the day, each night's sleep was a welcome release from the stress. All I could think about was the increasing debt we were in. I often contemplated suicide, only holding back because I couldn't leave my sons.

During this time, I began to pray to God and go to church. I found such comfort in my prayers but our circumstances continued to worsen. We did our best to hide the way things were but eventually I spoke to my vicar and he gave me John's phone number.

I telephoned John and he was so kind and compassionate. He didn't judge but just offered a helping hand. He came the next day and for the first time we looked at the whole situation. It had been too frightening before and I had stopped opening letters. I knew what was in them anyway!

John worked out a budget for us. He gave us a simple account book and showed me how to balance all our essential living costs – including the luxury of weekly food money! I still use this system today. He also spoke to all of our creditors and arranged a repayment plan that we could maintain.

Within a very short space of time our lives changed dramatically. No more picking the phone up with that awful sinking feeling, no more dreading the postman!

John advised me to tell my children that things were going to get better. They were six and eight years old by now and had only known a penny – pinching mum. I foolishly thought they might not understand but I will never forget the joy and relief on their faces. They have seen God's hand in changing our lives and are growing into young men I am incredibly proud of.

Over the next couple of years I supported John by writing to him and going to churches with him to give testimony of what God had done in my life through CAP.

Once our finances had stabilised, I found that I could live rather than just survive. We enjoyed simple things again like going to the cinema or to the swimming baths. Our home was a nice place to be instead of being filled with tension.

In 1998, I was stunned and delighted to be asked to become a Trustee for the charity. This was a great honour, especially having been involved in the charity from the start. It has continually chal-

lenged my faith and encouraged me to seek God and to grow personally. I am in awe of what God has done, is doing and will do in the future. We have so many wonderful people who have joined the staff. It is a pleasure to serve them and count them as friends. We see clients come to us in such great need and then see their lives transformed. It is amazing beyond words. I feel so blessed to be involved.

As CAP has grown it has lost none of the heart of love and grace. That is something that John and Lizzie planted right at the beginning and it increases as we increase.

Debbie and John outside Parliament 2000

In January 2002, I became involved in organising the prayer for the Charity becoming the National Prayer Co-ordinator in October of the same year. I know that this job is part of my destiny and I am humbled by the fact that God fulfilled this despite me making such a mess of my life for so long! I have so much I enjoy now, my home is peaceful, my children have fun, we get on well together, I love my job. Life just gets better and better, it has changed beyond recognition, as have I. It has been an incredible journey so far and I am so excited about what the future holds. What God is creating in and through CAP is very special and we are privileged to be a part of it, but more than that it's the relationships that are being forged as we go forward in God's will.

Debbie Thompson

National Prayer Co-ordinator and Second-ever CAP client.

CHAPTER FIVE

GOD SPEAKS: "DO NOT BE DISCOURAGED"

As 1996 drew to an end I started writing my diary, never for one minute thinking anyone else would ever read it.

December 31, 1996

As I look out from my bedroom office at home over a very snowy and cold Bradford, I am somehow overcome by many feelings and thoughts. What does 1997 hold for us? How will we cope emotionally and financially? What will happen to CAP?

These are just a few of my concerns as I look forward into 1997. I always think it is important to state where we are and what difficulties we face. It helps me put things into perspective and shows me how hopeless my circumstances would be were it not for the Lord working in every area of my life. It also helps to remind me that without His grace, guidance and provision I would be nowhere.

Our personal situation is very difficult indeed. We are two-and-a-half months behind with our mortgage. Although the building society has been understanding, we know that if by April this year we are unable to have some possibility of maintaining the mortgage payment we will be forced to sell the house. I bought it back in 1989 for £125,000 and I have tried to

sell it twice with no success. It is probably worth less than the
mortgage, which is £112,000 with interest being added. Losing
the house is something I have faced before and although
it would be a traumatic event the most important thing for me
would be that I could see that the Lord moved us on, not that
we lost the house. I am also very concerned how my wonderful
wife Lizzie and in particular my two girls Jasmine and Jessica
would cope with the loss of their home. We need another £800
per month just to pay the bills and remaining debts. Where will
this income of £1,600 per month come from?

I am also very disappointed and upset at the lack of support
we have received for the charity. In real terms, it is our only
source of income other than Lizzie's small wage, which just
feeds us each month. We have only a guaranteed monthly
income of £155 and we have just sent 500 newsletters out
before Christmas and as yet the response has been very small.
So many people seem oblivious to our plight and seem unable
to give us even the smallest amount of financial support. These
are people who have known us for years, Christians and
non-Christians who seem unable to even ask us how we are
managing or how the work is going on. I need God's grace and
understanding of this. Both of us take this lack of interest so
hard. We have written to more than 80 churches in the
Bradford area and only two churches have supported us: my
home church, Christian Life Church and Church on the Way.
We were astonished though by the financial support we
received from one Church of England vicar. I have written to
more than 100 large companies in Bradford asking for some
support and only two have offered any help: Empire Stores and
Seabrook Crisps. Only about 15 people have helped, if only they
knew how much it means to us.

Four such people spring to mind: Charles Barber, Janet
Green, Derek Gardiner and Olga Pochibko. These four people

don't really know us, had not even met us and knew nothing of our true plight but have supported us. We pray they will know just how much it has meant to us and it is through their actions and people like them that the Lord has confirmed his commitment to us. However, with such an overall weight of problems, why do we carry on? There are only two reasons. The first is for the people who we are helping through CAP. I only have to look at the files and think of the people to know that what we are doing is right from the Lord's heart to these people.

Each one was in a desperate situation of real oppression and poverty and just to think of individuals being able to buy food for their children, still having a roof over their heads and relationships being touched by the Lord is reason enough to keep going. Any price we have to pay is bearable just to know that people are being helped and when I look out of my window over Bradford I know that there are hundreds if not thousands of other families who are right now suffering poverty and oppression through debt. If we can help one hundred families in 1997 then let all the honour, praise and glory go to the Father. Which brings me on to the second and most important reason to carry on; that I believe with all my heart that this is God's will.

I have just spent this morning re-reading some of the scriptures that the Lord has laid on my heart for CAP and for continuing:

"Speak up for those who cannot speak for themselves, for the rights of all who are destitute. Speak up and judge fairly; defend the rights of the poor and needy."   *(Proverbs 31:8–9)*

You have been a refuge for the poor, a refuge for the needy in his distress, a shelter from the storm and a shade from the heat. For the breath of the ruthless is like a storm driving against a wall and like the heat of the desert.   *(Isaiah 25:4)*

"The Spirit of the Lord is on me, because he has anointed me to preach good news to the poor. He has sent me to proclaim freedom for the prisoners and recovery of sight for the blind, to release the oppressed, to proclaim the year of the Lord's favour."

(Luke 4:18–19)

. . . "Be strong and courageous, and do the work. Do not be afraid or discouraged, for the Lord God, my God, is with you. He will not fail you or forsake you until all the work for the service of the temple of the Lord is finished . . ."

(I Chronicles 28:20; given to me September 6, 1996)

Therefore, since we have been justified through faith, we have peace with God through our Lord Jesus Christ, through whom we have gained access by faith into this grace in which we now stand. And we rejoice in the hope of the glory of God. Not only so, but we also rejoice in our sufferings, because we know that suffering produces perseverance; perseverance, character; and character, hope. And hope does not disappoint us, because God has poured out his love into our hearts by the Holy Spirit, whom he has given us.

(Romans 5:1–5; given to me September 19, 1996)

Consider it pure joy, my brothers, whenever you face trials of many kinds, because you know that the testing of your faith develops perseverance. Perseverance must finish its work so that you may be mature and complete, not lacking anything. If any of you lacks wisdom, he should ask God, who gives generously to all without finding fault, and it will be given to him. But when he asks, he must believe and not doubt, because he who doubts is like a wave of the sea, blown and tossed by the wind. That man should not think he will receive anything from the Lord; he is a double-minded man, unstable in all he does.

The brother in humble circumstances ought to take pride in his high position. But the one who is rich should take pride in his low position, because he will pass away like a wild flower.

> For the sun rises with scorching heat and withers the plant; its blossom falls and its beauty is destroyed. In the same way, the rich man will fade away even while he goes about his business.
>
> Blessed is the man who perseveres under trial, because when he has stood the test, he will receive the crown of life that God has promised to those who love him.
>
> *(James 1:2–12; given to me September 19, 1996)*

When I re-read these wonderful words of encouragement they are almost the last word for all of us in CAP. In 1 Chronicles 11 v 4b–5 it describes David's attitude: "The Jebusites who lived there said to David 'You will not get in here'. Nevertheless, David captured the fortress of Zion, the city of David". He must have understood God's heart and decided to carry on. It was the same for us: that "nevertheless" attitude, only comes from knowing God is with you.

The word of God has both sustained us and encouraged us. I would often spend time with God asking Him for advice and encouragement. I would read daily devotionals and listen to other preachers. Whenever I felt in my spirit that a word was specifically for me or CAP, I noted it. At the end of the book you can see an appendix of the words given, the date, and who gave them to me. There is also a brief summary of circumstances surrounding me at the time.

The words of encouragement I received through the Bible stand as a testimony to God's amazing grace. Without His faithfulness and miraculous provision in terms of strength, determination and the sheer will to go on, we would have crumbled.

As you read the entry for the end of January you will see many of the ongoing struggles we faced then and throughout the whole seven years of CAP: lack of support; lack of encouragement; lack of appreciation; not knowing what to do but just carrying on regardless. We were doing everything in faith that the Lord would turn all things for the good because we love Him.

January 22, 1997

This weekend's sponsored walk along the canal at Shipley, was a real example of something we are beginning to realise is to be an on-going battle. How will we cope with lack of support?

Not one of the 14 people who we are helping came to the walk or rang to see how it went or even raised any sponsorship, however small. I found this very difficult as I have given so much into each situation, and I expected some help. However, as always, it revealed something I needed and will always need to deal with and that is: do I help people expecting them to understand the cost I pay and respond, or do I do it because it is right, and the Lord has called me to help? This has been a very interesting time and of course I have had to reaffirm that my calling is to help people irrespective of whether they appreciate it. I want to help them and show them God's love.

The issue of clients responding to our work has, over the years, been crucial. We have seen that clients who are grateful and who want to express this in some way are the ones more open to the Lord Jesus. Gratefulness expressed outwardly, e.g. sending letters of thanks, coming in to help with mail shots, fold newspapers or giving financially back into the charity, however small all show the same thing – a heart that wants to respond. Such a heart quickly warms to the love of Jesus.

January 22, 1997 continued

On the other hand, I was so encouraged by a friend named Paul Cribb who ran the whole way and raised £100; and Sheila – a brand new member of our Church – walked and raised some money. Steven and Karen Mason brought their two sons and walked all the way.

We also sent out 250 letters regarding the Awareness Evening and asked for more regular support, again only one person responded with some regular sponsorship and nothing from so many people. I now feel that I don't need to beg any more and that if people don't want to support us then that's fine and I should not put any more pressure on them. A few more people have come forward after our awareness evening which over 30 people attended. We now have two more regular givers and another two on the way.

These supporters are what we now call 'life changers' and it's interesting to note that despite very little encouragement, I somehow knew that it was right to just keep asking and to never stop developing regular individual financial support. We now have more than 1,200 'life changers' who, with gift aid, bring in over £18,000 per month (just over 20% monthly of our needs). God bless every one who has sown into the ministry. Every pound has encouraged us and still does. It keeps us sharp in terms of making sure our work is relevant to people and that they are prepared to continue to support us.

January 22, 1997 continued

The last two days have been some of the most traumatic regarding our financial situation. My attempts to come to agreements with my creditors have become more and more difficult. . . . Our financial situation is this: in three months we will need £1600 per month in income to stay in our house, keep up my debt payments and pay our bills.

While praying this morning and feeling I was at the end of my ability to cope the phone rang. It was Angela Spencer from church. She rang simply to say God had told her to ring and that I should not give up, and to read Joshua 1:9: "Have I not commanded you? Be strong and courageous. Do not be terrified, do not be discouraged, for the Lord your God will be with you wherever you go."

I also read Matthew 5:24-25: "Therefore everyone who hears these words of mine and puts them into practice is like a wise man who built his house on the rock. The rain came down, the streams rose, and the winds blew and beat against the house; yet it did not fall because it had its foundations on the rock."

To be honest, the wind is stronger than I had expected, the waves are bigger and more powerful and I am weaker than I had hoped. But I know we are built upon 'The Rock' and as His word says: "Yet it did not fall, because it had its foundation on the rock."

My friend Paul Hubbard came this morning and we were able to pray and believe that the Lord was in control and that I had a job to do. I was lifted in faith. I am determined to continue.

Paul has been there for me so many times over the years. He has always been able to stand with me, to express his faith in God, in me and that we will get through. He probably has no idea just how grateful we have been so many times for his encouragement and commitment to us. He is so strong in the Lord and the Word. He is a wonderful man of God and I consider myself privileged to know him.

January 28, 1997

Over the weekend the building society called and stated that they would not accept my request for a couple of months to try and sort things out and they would start proceedings and action to, as they put it, "protect their interests". After much prayer we decided that today we would put our wonderful house up for sale. We are three months behind with our mortgage. We believe that God will provide for us but if He has any other ideas or plans then we want to remain open. I will put a sign up in faith that if God wants to keep us in this house He is big enough to do it and provide the money in time.

I feel a bit like Abraham when God said sacrifice your son. I am not suggesting that I would be able to do anything which remotely resembled that act of faith but I feel that giving my wife, children, house, reputation and life into the Lord's hands I am left with nothing but the Lord.

It's times like this that you are tempted and really wonder what is happening to you. A credit card company, who I still owe money to, rang up and simply said: "Give us our money!". No compassion, only insults and suggestions that I should go and get a proper job. Income support said unless I was prepared to sign a contract saying I would seek alternative employment then they would not help us in any way. I can't lie just to get money, my God is bigger than that.

My wonderful wife is beside me and I feel so much for her facing our first year of marriage with an uncertain future, not knowing where we might end up. Her support and belief in me is beyond my understanding.

Two people touched me today in all the difficulties. One was my friend Avril who said we could stay in her caravan in the garden if we lost the house. Her compassion for us was unbelievable. It has only just sunk in that homelessness is a possibility. Am I prepared to put my words and faith into action and continue with CAP and the ministry work, if that is the price we have to pay?

The others, Chris and Mark our friends and supporters, said

they would make a monthly donation. They believe in us and know our situation.

January 28, 1997 continued

I have been thinking of my over-all situation. My children are asleep upstairs and Lizzie is out and I have wept in my office. When I think about our circumstances and of what we might have to go through, I can feel myself saying: "No Lord, this is just too much to take."

What can I say? I am a broken man. All the rejection, the lack of support, the relentless pressure and uncertainty seems too much to bear.

Yet I just have to think of Dennis and Denise, Debbie Thompson and Carl and many of the people I have helped and will help. I know I have no option but to carry on. Something deep within me says "this is the way son, trust Me, I will not let you down I understand your tears and fears and I will store them up for my future glory". I am trying to be strong as Joshua was commanded but I am falling short. I need the Lord more now than at any time in my life. I have nothing else to hold on to.

I must carry on. People need me tomorrow. I have a funding document to complete, a life to live and a wife and children who need me. I pray that the Lord will meet me just where I am in this situation of destitution and need. I know He will and that somehow He will find a way in the darkness. Over recent weeks I have been going to Church on the Way, Bradford to listen to Charles Price. He is a great bible teacher and has been speaking on 'Treasures in the Darkness'. To be honest, it feels like it doesn't get much darker than this and I just know that there are treasures as yet unseen in this darkness. Praise God.

I hope you can get the sense from what I wrote that it was God and God alone who was holding me up at this time. There was just something inside me that said I will not stop, I can't stop whatever the cost. I feel somewhat embarrassed that I used examples such as Abraham to describe how I was feeling.

What follows is an amazing proclamation of what I believed was the beginning of the unstoppable spirit that the Lord had born in us. I think this was one of the darkest times for me. However, from this point things began to really get moving. William Spencer, who was in our church, volunteered to help one day a week. He was to join full-time in September. He was the first in an ever-growing list of men and women who have shown incredible support and sacrifice to help me see God's vision become a reality.

February 26, 1997.

What a month! Over the last four weeks I have been totally consumed with completing our funding document and our new promotional video with a good friend, Malcolm West. Last Friday I completed a mail shot letting people know what we are doing. Well the situation is now as they say on the edge! We now face a very desperate financial situation. All the money that CAP has and some it doesn't even have, has been swallowed up with the £1,000 cost of the funding document. This has meant that I have only received £200 over the last eight weeks and it went towards my mortgage.

I have basically reached the end of the road financially; four months arrears on my mortgage, £400 needed in the next week for bills, and debts with virtually nothing left.

A promised £750 gift has not come in and I just don't know which way to turn. Yet again the response to the 300 letters sent out has been very poor – only six responses and three of them were asking to be taken off the mailing list! Yet again I am faced with the reality that many people just don't understand or are not sufficiently moved to help. Although we have another two supporters, we only have a total regular monthly income of £275.

When I sit and think over the last year, since I left my job, I can sense the enemy pulling on my emotions, that people don't believe in me, for instance only five people attended my seminar last night. One person whom I am helping and who faces enormous problems rang up and said they were a 'bit tired' so wouldn't be coming. I was a 'bit tired' I had worked since 8am and would not finish until 11pm. Will this constant and unbelievable pressure on my finances ever go away? Am I destined to a life of unsupported ministry?

Can I carry on paying the price if CAP is destined to remain small and we are only going to help a small number of people? If I am to have my house repossessed and be destitute and in debt for the rest of my life, would I carry on? The honest answer is that I don't feel that I could do that. The reasons are partly my lack of faith in my ability to sustain how I live for a long period of time but secondly I know that my God will not allow that to happen. When absolutely nothing you can see confirms what the Lord has said to you, you are left only with His word and promises.

I believe that the Lord will provide for us, that we will not live a destitute life, that my debts will be cleared, that CAP will grow to be a wonderful ministry helping thousands of people. I see a time when we will be blessed financially and that I will have a reasonable income and be able to afford to live, pay my bills and have a decent life for my wife and children. I can feel my spirits lifted by simply writing these truths down and the enemy has no defence against the promises of God.

All I have to do is carry on – that's my responsibility. The rest is up to God. I am left not knowing what will happen but knowing God cares and it will be Him who sees us through, supports us, encourages us and ultimately provides for our needs.

April 11, 1997

Over the last six weeks, things have really got going as far as the ministry is concerned. We are now taking on about one or two new families per week and the results are incredible. People are becoming Christians and it is a real honour and privilege to see how God is using me to minister His grace, love and compassion.

As far as finances and funding are concerned, we have had the best month ever in March. Nearly £2,000 came in and I got paid enough to actually put something towards my mortgage. I have just read Loren Cunningham's book *Living on the Edge* and it has been a revelation to me. He was the one who started YWAM, (Youth With A Mission) a huge international Christian ministry working with young people to affect the world around them. He never gave up. God eventually and supernaturally, met all his needs and grew the ministry into the world-wide organisation it is today.

This book was a great source of encouragement to me and it was one of the motivations to write this book. My hope is that someone starting out in ministry may one day read *Nevertheless* and if they are even half as encouraged, challenged and inspired as I was with his book, then that will be wonderful.

April 11, 1997 continued

I have had several tempting opportunities that would have allowed me to get my finances back under control. One was a part-time job and the other was the idea of commercially using the services and products we have developed to make money.

I felt a little uneasy and I have had it confirmed by a recent trustees meeting that God is in control not me. The ministry work is more than full time and that's where God wants me. If I went down these new avenues I would only try to take back control instead of believing in His provision.

Our personal circumstances continue to get worse. As far as our home is concerned, we received the dreaded letter from the building society saying the account was to be transferred to the collection and recovery department, i.e. repossession action was to be started. Both Lizzie and myself are strangely calm about it all. We realise that God doesn't need a letter from the building society to tell him how much arrears we are in. His plans and purposes are not suddenly altered by a letter.

Having said that, someone is coming to look round our beautiful house tomorrow. All the concern about where we might live and whether we are really going to be asked to give up our home, suddenly becomes a reality.

Today I was introduced to David Evans from Tear Fund, a huge international Christian relief agency working mainly in the third world, who might be able to help with funding. I find myself wondering what is God trying to tell me. Why am I unable to pay the mortgage? Why doesn't anybody just send us a cheque for £10,000? William (Spencer) got a great deal of insight into this "wilderness experience" we are going through. He felt the Lord say that "A seed which receives no water will only survive if it sends its root deep underground trying to find the water. The eventual tree that results is strong and fully able to use the rains when they come. God needs to ensure that we will be able to manage what He has for us."

Is our character right? Have we lost our own pride? Are we really able to rely totally on Him? Are we prepared to pay the price? These are very difficult questions. However, not for one minute do I doubt that we have been called by God, that the ministry is right from the heart of God and that He will see us through.

I get a sense that I need to just rest in His arms and stop trying to work it out. I must rest in the certain knowledge that all things work to the good of those who love the Lord. I am also reminded of Matthew 6 v 25– 34 that tells us not to worry. At the end it says: "Seek first His kingdom and righteousness and all these things will be given to you as well."

I pray that God will help me to keep my eyes focused on Him as I would surely sink if I looked at my circumstances and the fact that it all seems impossible. It's a bit like Peter, when he walked on the water then sank when he took his eyes off Jesus. I also realise that as he sank, Jesus held him and he was safe.

April 28, 1997

The work continues with more and more examples of God's grace and the fact that CAP can, has and will make a huge difference in people's lives. I feel somewhat isolated as if nobody else can see what I can see. When will it all end? I have to stop now as David Evans from Tear Fund has just arrived.

April 29, 1997

A very good day with David Evans yesterday. He was very impressed by our work and I took him to see three of the people I am helping. He can't guarantee anything but there is hope that they may be able to fund us with up to £10,000! We won't know until about the end of May but praise God: a small breakthrough.

I had a call from the building society today as well and basically if we don't get the funding before the end of May they have no option but to begin the process of repossessing our home. I feel strangely calm. It looks as if the Lord is either going to take us to the wire or He has somewhere else for us to live.

It's at times like this when my mind works overtime wondering what will come next and how we will cope. Am I missing something? Is there anything else I could do?

I have often spoken out that we were prepared to pay the price of our financial security and our home. It's all so easy to say but what a difference when it looms before you as a reality. It really tests your faith and belief in what you are doing. All the old chestnuts of not understanding people's lack of support have surfaced all over again. Should we share our plight, is there any point in us continuing the fight for our home?

The uncertainty is killing me. If only I knew, I could begin to plan but the Lord obviously has a reason for this uncertainty. If He wants to know if I am serious, He surely must realise that I will give my life for Him and the vision He has given me. I know He knows that, so why the test? Why the wait? Why the anguish?

I have just read Psalm 91. What a word!

v2: "I will say of the Lord: 'He is my refuge and my fortress, my God, in whom I trust.'"

v4: "He will cover you with His feathers and under His wing you will find refuge, His faithfulness will be your shield and rampart."

vv14–15: "'Because he loves me,' says the Lord, 'I will rescue him; I will protect him, for he acknowledges my name. He will call upon me and I will answer him. I will be with him in trouble, I will deliver him and honour him.'"

Praise God for His word just in time! I know that I was born for such a time as this. This ministry is God's work. It is right out of His word. He will sustain me, He will uphold us because it says so. I have nothing else to hang onto except His word and I will not let go of the calling or His promises.

I hope the following extract will bring home to you what it feels like when you owe someone money and they are constantly wanting more and you have no more to give. I had debts from my past and had arranged with each creditor except one to accept reduced monthly payments. One company refused to understand and they had continued to hassle me. I was reaching breaking point. It's these types of experiences that the Lord has used to give me a real compassion and drive to help the many thousands of people who face the same situations.

May 3, 1997

10.30am.

Yesterday morning, Saturday, just as we were setting off for a day out with the girls the phone rang. It was the same credit card collection company. The lady on the other end of the phone simply carried on where they left off last time they spoke to me and she simply demanded more money. As I explained my plight, at the end of each exchange she simply stated that £10.00 per month was not enough. I explained I was on a very low income, not eligible for any benefit and had been paying without missing for five years. Even when I explained that I was facing losing my home over the next few weeks, had no regular income, that I was running a Christian charity working to help the poor she simply said: "More money or we will take you to court!"

It is important to understand that having worked in the finance industry for 17 years, I know that the company would get nothing if they took me to court. I know I have been totally honourable in all my financial affairs. However, this lady made me feel like dirt! Not for the first time throughout the last five years her attitude and threats almost brought me to my knees. What was I supposed to do? I have to admit I finally lost it. I just could not talk to this lady and the feelings of helplessness, injustice and vulnerability were too much to bear. I had to ask her to ring me on Tuesday when I would be able to talk better and I have to admit I put the phone down.

Now, I am not a man who can't fight his corner but she finally ground me down so much that I basically cracked. After the telephone conversation I could hardly speak to Lizzie, and she was unwell. She suffers from some sort of stomach problem, where she is physically sick for about two days. The doctors don't know what it is even though she has had it investigated. However, she knew what pain I felt and utter desperation and dejection. Somehow we were able to pick ourselves up and go for a day out with some wonderful Christian friends Chris and Mark who paid for our day out at Harewood House.

Throughout the day I kept feeling so down about everything. I alone know the true extent of our financial situation, we need £250 over the next week to keep going. The Lord was so good to me. He picked me up and somehow we had a great day and I hope none of the friends who were with us would have known how I was feeling.

Today, Sunday, Lizzie is unwell again and although I try to keep her aware of what is happening I don't burden her if I feel nothing would be helped by her worrying as well.

The *Word For Today* for the last three days has been a great source of encouragement for me. Friday's word was "Patience is the bridge that carries you from the will of God to the promises of God". It went on "If you do the will of God on this side, the promises are waiting for you on the other". The key point was this: "Bridges come in different lengths and only God knows how long they are". The question asked was: "Are you doing the will of God?" I have to say, as far as I am aware, we are doing the will of God.

The second question was: "Are you walking patiently and confidently before the Lord in this matter?" I am convinced that we are on a bridge with a definite and glorious end, I don't know how long it is or how rough it will get but I know, with God's help and the faith He has given me, we will get to the other side. I just pray it's not too long and we will still be around to enjoy the other side.

Yesterday spoke of Mark 14 v 8 "She has done what she could" and went on to state the words of Edmund Burke who said "Nobody ever made a greater mistake than he who did nothing because he could only do a little."

I feel so overwhelmed by the size of my problems and the magnitude by which things are out of my control. I am a practical man, a man who has not relied on anyone, someone who is willing to give his all for what he believes. However, I have never realised just how insignificant I am against my situation and problems. I am doing what I can, I continue to serve and be faithful in the small things.

I Corinthians 1:27: "But God chose the foolish things of the world to shame the wise; God chose the weak things of the world to shame the strong."

I have decided that I am going to use all the God-given gifts I have to take on this credit card collection company. I will start on Tuesday at the local county court to see if I can, with the Lord's guidance and help, take these people to court and see if I can win justice for my case. In the long run it would also create a precedent where companies will be forced to accept a reasonable and just offer of debt repayment. I can imagine what the result of that would bring in the work we undertake. I am encouraged by many proverbs that speak of the Lord helping and supporting the lowly in court.

Proverbs 22:22: "Do not exploit the poor because they are poor and do not crush the needy in court, for the Lord

will take up their case and will plunder those who plunder
them."

Proverbs 16:19: "Better to be lowly in spirit and among the
oppressed than to share plunder with the proud."

Proverbs 17:5: "He who mocks the poor shows contempt
for their Maker; whoever gloats over disaster will not go
unpunished."

Although I did not know it, this was the start of CAP's insolvency
service. This desperate five-year battle with this debt collection
company would eventually give me the knowledge to help other
people facing huge debt. Only God could use such circumstances
for good. We now have a specialist insolvency service, which has
helped hundreds of families facing similar insurmountable repayment of debt.

May 3, 1997 continued

Today's *Word For Today* is Psalm 91:15: "He will call upon me,
and I will answer him; I will be with him in trouble, I will deliver
him and honour him."

The general point was that if you were in trouble then God
was right in the middle of it with you. A simple point but how
true and what a comfort!

Genesis 39:20: "But while Joseph was in prison the Lord was
with him" Joseph was in prison for a crime he didn't commit.

I feel like I am in a prison but I know God is with me in this
prison. Paul when writing to the church at Philippi while he was
actually in prison or more likely under house arrest in Philippians
4:12–13 he said:

"I know what it is to be in need, and I know what it is to have
plenty. I have learned the secret of being content in any and

every situation, whether well fed or hungry, whether living in plenty or in want. I can do everything through Him who gives me strength."

As we face such an uncertain time, I feel very much encouraged to think of the future glory the Lord will receive through our witness and the success of the ministry. He will also be glorified by the difficult times we will have managed. All of a sudden the 28 days to our year end, when I need so much, seems a different proposition. I have just realised God knows how long we have to go because He is right here with us. Also our pressing and urgent needs are God's needs because He is here with us living within us and He knows exactly what we need. Praise God for His word and the faithfulness of people and organisations like United Christian Broadcasting who publish *Word For Today*.

May 10, 1997

Today is an example of the different set of emotions that I face on a daily basis. First of all, my insecurities and weaknesses have been exposed by the way both Lizzie and myself are pulling apart rather than together in our situations. We got into a real state over what I should wear at some friends' wedding. It wiped me out all last night and then again this morning.

Then I opened the mail and on one hand got £500 from the William Brooke Benevolent Fund, praise God! Then the very next letter was from the building society refusing my, totally in faith, offer on my mortgage. They were giving me 14 days or they will pass my account to collection and recoveries. The next letter was from Tear Fund saying it would take about two months before anything could be arranged. My great hope of immediate financial support is gone. The pressure of the ministry workload I face is great and I am just falling behind all the time. I feel very lonely and isolated as if by choice I have shut myself away and I have virtually closed down.

Praise God that I have Him to fall back on. He knows my needs and He has provided the essential requirements like food and He will continue. Why no future financial resource? I am unable to explain how I feel. I am like the three Lepers in 2 Kings 7. They were outside the gates of Samaria in a desert. Inside the city there was a great famine, people were eating their own children and spending thousands of pounds on a donkey head to eat! These lepers were outcasts from their own people and as they looked round they were surrounded by the army of Ben-Hadad which had laid siege to Samaria.

2 Kings 7:3–4: "Why stay here until we die?" If we say, 'We'll go into the city' – the famine is there, and we will die. And if we stay here, we will die. So let us go over to the camp of the Arameans and surrender. If they spare us, we live, if they kill us we die."

I feel like those lepers, every way I can go looks like certain death. If I give up I'm finished. If I stop I'm finished. I only have one option and that is to carry on and if I fail I will fail trying and if I'm finished then so be it. I've nearly had enough. "Nevertheless" I will just carry on whatever.

I am encouraged that God went ahead of the lepers and performed miracles before their very eyes and the army fled and they just could not believe what they found in the enemy camp – abundance for themselves. They immediately relieved the siege of Samaria and all the people were released from the famine. There are many parallels with my situation but I can't yet see the miracles. However, I know that God goes before me and my only task is to keep going forward with His calling and know that God is with me.

In chapter 7:2 there is an officer who speaks out his doubts. He never saw the glory of God. I know that there are doubters of the vision and calling I have. As Elisha said, there would be a lifting of the siege, I pray that none will miss the end of the vision God has given me. I pray I will be sustained by His power throughout this period of need and uncertainty.

Our first year ended and what a year it had been. We had got the charity up and running and we had proved that we could change lives. People were becoming Christians! It had been a massive test and struggle but we were as convinced as ever that we were on the right track. We had seen 79 people and had a total income of just £10,413 but we were underway. What would the second year hold for us all?

June 1, 1997

We are waiting to hear whether our house will be repossessed. We have just survived the last three weeks on a gift from someone I really did not expect to give us anything.

It's strange what things cause me difficulties; it's not the big things, it's the little things. Like not being able to get the picture frame I wanted for one of my paintings. Yet we manage every week. It's the constant need and uncertainty that tends to grind you down. As soon as one thing is paid, another is due. You constantly have no knowledge of where it will come from. Next week is a great example. We need some money for petrol and a day out with the children tomorrow, let's say £30. We still owe £30 for Lizzie's bridesmaid dress, £50 for next weekend, £90 to pay the bills by the 10th, £140 for our debt repayments by the 15th and then the mortgage. Currently we have virtually nothing either in any bank or our house. We have been here many times.

I have been getting a sense that God is about to open up the floodgates and provision is about to flow. Joshua and the

miraculous crossing of the Jordan has really lifted me. The
Word for Today says "Are you expectant of the miraculous
intervention of God?" and I am.

I believe that within the next month we will see God's
provision for CAP and the house will be saved. God will provide
enough for William (Spencer) to join me and we will be able to
move forward and really get CAP going. I see £50,000 to
£60,000 being released and then everybody will know the
support God has shown us throughout the last year.

It's wonderful how God can lift your eyes from what you see
to what you know. He can lift your spirit so much. As Philippians
3 says: "And the peace of God which transcends all
understanding will guard your hearts and minds in Christ Jesus."

I pray that the next time I write, it will be to record
God's abundant blessing on the ministry and our financial
situation.

It is strange to read of this almost unexplainable confidence and
expectant faith God had given me. I obviously knew that everything was going to be all right. It is also obvious to me that at this
very dark time I had the grace of God for what I was facing. I
was about three months early in my timing and a few thousand
pounds out but there was a sense from deep within me that something was about to break. Praise God for His grace when we need
it most.

June 6, 1997

A very tough week. The pressure continues to build but the
Lord continues to provide on a daily basis. On Sunday we
were given £50 by Jan, a former client, and that money
allowed us to go out with the girls on Monday. Today we got
another £100, which will pay for the bridesmaid dress and our

weekend. We also realised that we had £24 in savings stamps for Morrisons the supermarket so we will be able to buy enough food for the next few days. Praise God for His provision. I continue to fundraise and have "cast my bread upon the water". I have sent over 70 requests for funding. All I can now do is pray and wait for God to move.

Lizzie and myself have had a good week reading Joshua and looking at God's promises and today I now know why. We received the letter from the building society asking us to pay £3,693.35 arrears on our mortgage. I am struck by how ridiculous our situation looks. Here I am praising God for the £24 we have got to buy our food and yet our mortgage and our house security look so unsure. Yet it is these times when the word becomes life. I'm not desperate about losing the house. I don't think we will and that's nothing to do with what I can see. Far from it, anybody else would say we have lost the house and we will become homeless! Yet I know deep down in my heart that we have been faithful and that the Lord has commanded a blessing upon us. All I have to do is be strong and courageous and wait for it to come. What will the next few weeks bring? Trials or provision? Yet I expect a miraculous intervention by God into our circumstances and that we will go away on our holiday on July 19 knowing that we are secure in our ministry and that the house is safe.

We have been invited to go on holiday to Wales with some good friends. All we need is a caravan/tent, some money and some time off. I sense that God has got it all in hand. All we have to do is have faith that God would want us to be restored, refreshed and enjoy a holiday. He will do the rest.

The girls have been drawing pictures of caravans and tents and they are praying that God will give us a mobile home or something similar for our family holiday. I'm so touched by their child-like faith and total trust that we will be all right. We never tell them about the true situation but we speak a little about possibly moving to somewhere smaller. They just seem to take it all in their stride.

June 7, 1997

Today we actually crossed a new border of our faith. We have got through the week but if we go out tonight as planned with friends, we have only £19 for food. Should I tell someone? Should I borrow from someone? Difficult decisions! I have decided not to tell anyone and Lizzie will use the money to get us through the weekend. I pray that something will come up on Monday as we need £90 for our council tax and water rates as well as some more food money.

Praise God for the faith He gives us! I don't feel too bad, I just know that God is faithful in all He promises and His word says in Psalm 37: "Never have I seen the children of the righteous begging bread." Amen.

I am so confident that God is faithful that I can now go out and play my part in our outreach today and tomorrow and I pray that more will come to know the Jesus whom I love and serve.

July 12, 1997

What a four weeks we have just had. Such highs and such lows. Firstly, the provision of a holiday for Lizzie, the girls and myself. We had no money, no caravan, tent, trailer or tow bar however we knew it was right despite our dire financial situation. The girls started to pray and we just knew God would make it happen. Well, over the last four weeks Avril and Chris Gray have not only offered us their wonderful caravan for two weeks but they will even tow it down to Wales and back! What generosity!

(Avril was the first to sow into CAP and they were the couple who said we could live in their back garden in their caravan if we had nowhere to live!)

We then needed money to cover the site costs, petrol and spending money etc. Some friends gave us £500 and said they would pay for our site fees. Words almost fail me when we see God meet our needs in such a dynamic way.

Our house and mortgage situation continue to be very difficult. We are now nearly £4000 in arrears and we have until the end of August – just 50 days – to give the building society some certainty we can pay the mortgage. The enormity of the problem in some ways takes away the worry as there is absolutely nothing we can do but keep working in the ministry.

We have had good support from ten Trusts over the last month and financially the Charity is in better shape than before but we still need £2,500 before the end of August to keep going.

I am still disappointed when people almost refuse to consider helping us. A Christian fund said they would not even consider our application because they felt we were not working across the whole church and that they would not give their support. The reason? "I was a one man band". Shame on them for their short-sightedness, what more could I do? I work with any church, any Christians irrespective of doctrine. We cut right across the church and six people have now come to know the Lord as a direct result of the ministry and the fund refuses to even consider helping us.

I agonised whether to keep this last entry in. I want to say that this particular fund has supported many excellent charities and projects over the years. I now have no doubt that I just did not fit their criteria. I left it in mainly to show how hard I found it and how desperate I was that people knew just what amazing work God was doing through us. At the time I felt like they were persecuting and rejecting me, which I now realise is nonsense.

July 12, 1997 continued

I am getting better overall with rejection (everything's relative, I suppose!) and the more I work with the people who come to me the more I know this is God's work and the responsibility for funding it is His. I don't have to worry about the overall future of the ministry. My one job is to be faithful in the small things and seek His will for the direction of the work.

Lizzie and I have been having some difficulties over the last month. I have been quite sharp with her. I sense that the pressure of a front line ministry has an impact on your closest relationships. God has to put me back on the right path!

After a six-year battle I finally won an amazing final victory over the one remaining credit card collection company that had given me such a hard time. When I started the legal action over their refusal to accept my offer, they said my action was wrong. However, they would now accept my offer. I have to pay just £10 a month for the next five years on a total debt of £3,000. With this final acceptance, I now only have to pay £7,000 on the £24,000 I owe. I remember in 1992 when everything collapsed I owed £78,000. To think that in five years I will have cleared everything is a huge relief. What a gracious and providing God!

Over the next five years we managed, somehow, to make every agreed repayment to my creditors and in May 2002, five years later, we paid our last repayment. What a faithful and awesome God we serve. I am grateful to all the finance companies which, eventually, accepted our offers. The feeling of being debt free, apart from mortgage and HP on my car, is one I am determined thousands of people will experience over the coming years as they work with CAP.

CHAPTER SIX

CAP's FIRST EMPLOYEES

A year into our work our perseverance was beginning to pay off. William Spencer handed in his notice and came to work for CAP as our first real employee.

August 14, 1997

Today just over a week since William gave his job up in faith to join me full time £5000 came from Trust for the Homeless! It is difficult to explain just what this means to us, we can get paid for the next two months. I feel our home is now safe.

I got to know Roger Carson, who headed the trust, quite well and I still don't think he understands just how much his faith in me meant and that his was the first trust to really believe in what we were doing. There will never be another morning quite like that morning when I opened that letter. It broke something. Praise God for men and women of God who have a heart to give.

August 14, 1997 continued

Then, while I was away on the 21st of August, Tudor Trust agreed a grant of £8000. I got the phone call from William and although I had been through so much and knew that God would meet my needs, I could not believe that we were going to be paid for the next few months and that CAP would, for the first time, have some financial base.

Just before we went away on holiday, we were given a word from Sue Kenny which she said she had seen a vision of a pillar of smoke over our house and it wasn't moving. She felt certain that God wanted us to stay in our house. I felt certain that God had granted us the house and although the situation was still very serious re the mortgage etc. I took the 'For Sale' sign down and managed to pay the full monthly mortgage payment for the first time in over a year. We went on holiday in faith that God would be working on the whole situation while we were away.

We had had a fantastic trustees meeting on July 24 where, in total faith, we stated that we wanted to pay William and myself as employees. At the time we had very little money, but we felt it was right to set salaries in faith and trust God.

For the last year, CAP was my only source of income and I had received only £4,000.

As I re-read these entries I am blown away by the magnitude of God's faithfulness to us. In just one month we went from no money and William giving his job up to join a ministry with a few hundred pounds, to literally thousands of pounds coming in. Amazing!

September 10, 1997

Things just get better! More finances have come in, we have seen God provide us with some computer equipment through the Lloyds TSB Foundation. Not just any old rubbish either – the very best and latest system that should be installed over the next couple of weeks.

The Lloyds TSB Foundation were to support us over the next six years and they continue to do so to this day.

> We have spent some time this week looking at Nehemiah and in particular how he defended the wall when it was half built. We felt that God was saying that for the next few weeks we had to defend what He had done so far. We decided that we needed to set things up for the future with more work on the computer systems and establishing the office.
>
> We also decided that we needed a new brochure, which would help with all our work in the future. What a feeling to know that you have time to get things right, that you are not chasing money all the time and trying to get the ministry growing in your own strength!
>
> We believe that we need to seek God's direction for CAP, we don't want to waste time going in the wrong direction. We need to allow God to bring the right people at the right time and we just need to be diligent, work hard and trust His ability to make things happen.
>
> Praise God for the wonderful outpouring of His provision and love for us and as I have always said it is that which makes the difference and without Him we would be absolutely nowhere.

September 16, 1997

> While at the Kings Park conference I received the following prophecy:
>
> "You have a deposit but you have much more to come into – bigger than even you can see now. Just keep walking into it, it's coming towards you. There is more to come!"
>
> Praise God for his confirmation of our work and direction.

Over the next three months things got going and we came into a new sense of God's provision. One thing that I notice, when I look back, is that even after such a traumatic first year we did not hold back at this time. We never said let's stop and stay where we are – we have the money for a few months. We just pressed on with looking for another full-time member of staff and growing the work. The next member of staff was to be Ruth Graves. Ruth worked at Lloyds TSB near our house and back in June 1996 when I paid the first £10 into the bank she was the cashier that took the money. She asked about CAP and she became a 'life changer' and always asked me about the work whenever I paid money in. She came to see what we did and then decided to give up her very secure job and join us. She left without any redundancy and was such a blessing to us. She was later to marry the Rev Charles Barber, then one of our Trustees, and they now have four beautiful children. When Ruth left to have the twins she became a Trustee and served as a woman of real faith and vision for many years finally stepping down in early 2003. All that from one paying-in slip and the question: "who are Christians Against Poverty?"

September 16, 1997 continued

Over the month of September we continued to receive more funding. Trust for the Homeless gave another £5,000! Roger Carson, who headed the Trust, said he was so touched by my thank you that he felt God tell him to send me another £5,000!

To this day this expression of generosity and faith in us stands almost alone. You have to remember there were only the two of us and we had only had £10,000 over the first twelve months. This man and his wonderful Trust doubled that in just two months. It was such an amazing gesture led by the Holy Spirit. Even so, it needed men and women of God to have faith that they had heard right, and generous hearts to actually send the money. Under God's guidance this Trust distributed its funds and closed in the late nineties. Roger remains a great supporter of the charity.

September 16, 1997 continued

The Tudor Trust money came in and we found ourselves with just over £13,000 in the bank. We needed two cars to visit clients and we decided that as Tear Fund were expected to give us £10,000 we would wait until it was confirmed on September 18.

However, the decision was delayed due to too many proposals on the meeting day and we would not find out until October 1. The choice was simple, wait or buy the cars we needed now. We really needed them now, we had only one car that was unreliable and we were travelling more and more. However, the cost of the cars was two-and-a-half months' salary and running costs. Praise God we chose the option of faith. We bought two cars and left ourselves with only £2,600 at the end of September – less than one month's money.

You will not be surprised that Tear Fund did agree to our grant and it came in during October and we continued to move forward in our work. We now had enough money for December and January. We also received notification from the Sir Halley Stewart Trust that they would fund us with £3,000 per quarter starting in January.

This trust was to become one of the most encouraging we have ever had. They supported us for six years right up to 2003. They broke the one rule many trusts have which is to only fund something for a short period of time. They became our friends and initially through Penny Fawcett, and now Sue West (trust administrators), they have really got to understand what we do. I pray they are pleased with our progress and that God will let them know just how much we have appreciated their continued support.

Tear Fund also supported us right up to last year. We have been so grateful to them for their involvement with us, and we very much look up to them as a standard to reach for, in how they operate as a Christian organisation.

This whole area of getting good equipment and hiring staff irrespective of whether you have the money is one thing that over the years has marked us out. We get the best computer systems we can. We never, to this date, make any purchase decision on whether we have the money. If we need it, we get it. We have the faith that God will meet our needs. The testimony to God's provision is that we have always been able to pay every invoice and bill, if a few days late on some occasions. We know the way God has led us has brought some criticism, but I can only remain true and faithful to how I feel God has called us to operate.

Time and time again God has helped us step out in faith. Over the years our trustees have again and again backed us with these decisions and not restricted what we need due to perceived lack of finance. This has meant that in practice we may have looked foolish and unwise but, believe me, if there had been another way, we would have done it. Faith to me is when you step out into the unknown. It is being certain of a future hoped for but not yet seen.

In our kitchen we have an *Every Day with Jesus* calendar, by Selwyn Hughes; and today's word, the 19th of January 2003, is the following: "Faith is . . . the conviction of things not seen" (Hebrews 11:1 RSV)

It also says: "We continue to meditate on the Bible's one and only definition of faith. Today we examine the second phrase in this definition; Faith is . . . the conviction of things not seen". It's easy to believe in things we can see, but not so easy to believe in the things we cannot see. Yet this is exactly where faith operates. We do not need faith to operate in the realm of things we can see; it is sight, not faith that operates there.

Faith operates in the realm of things the physical eye cannot see, and is able, as the writer to the Hebrews puts it, to "see the invisible". This is not a contradiction, but a paradox. A paradox is something that may seem contrary to reason, but nevertheless is true.

Faith is a paradox. Faith sees the invisible, knows the unknowable, hears the inaudible, touches the intangible – fights in chains, and rests in conflict. Contradictory? No – paradoxical *and* therefore true.

Hebrews 11:1: "Now faith is being sure of what we hope for and certain of what we do not see." v6 "And without faith it is impossible to please God, because anyone who comes to him must believe that He exists and that He rewards those who earnestly seek him."

November 22, 1997

Today we received an acceptance letter from Ruth Graves in answer to our job offer. Again what faith God has given us! Here we are with only two month's money, no sign of any great outpouring of finance and we have agreed to offer a job to Ruth. What is even more spectacular is that she knows that we have no funding at present but is prepared to give up her job at the bank, where she has worked for 11 years, to work for us.

Here are some of the quotes from her letter.

The first thing is that God has specifically called me to work alongside you in your ministry. God has prepared me to join CAP. As far as finances go, I do understand the "faith" element

that the ministry operates in. In fact I wouldn't want it any
other way. I look forward to seeing God provide for our needs.
I know that God is true to His word Phil 4:19: "and my God
will meet all your needs in His glorious riches in Christ Jesus".
I will have no hesitation in handing in my notice on the 1st of
January even if my redundancy does not come through.

She ended her letter with Ephesians 3:20–21 "Now to Him who
is able to do immeasurably more than all we ask, or imagine,
according to His power that is at work within us, to Him be
glory . . ."
   Psalm 27:14: "Wait for the Lord; be strong and take heart
and wait for the Lord."

This has to be one of the most amazing job acceptance letters
ever. I can just feel her total faith that God was in her decision
and that it was her destiny to join CAP. We need to remember that at
this time it was just a very small ministry with two blokes working from a bedroom office in a house that looked like it still could
be repossessed. Outstanding faith or what?

November 27, 1997

Over the last few days Caroline Bateman has come to see us
and it can only be God who has brought her. Together with her
husband, she has supported us from the beginning and didn't
really know us. She feels that God is calling her into our ministry
and she is obviously talented and well able to be a great blessing
to our ministry. The only problem is that again we are looking at
hiring someone to add a quarter to our staff, take our monthly
expenses up to £7,000 and we have only just enough to pay
William and myself until the end of January at the most.
   On top of all that we have heard that our application for
funding from Bradford Council has been turned down for

something about our constitution. They just didn't want to fund us.

On the other hand Franco Fotti, who is a friend of ours from Cleveland, Ohio who ministers in Italy, was with us on Tuesday night and gave us the following prophecy:

> God starts at the end – He knows the end from the beginning. Your ministry will be talked about in every paper in the land. You will come before kings and rulers.
>
> You will pour out blessings and abundance, not because of you but because of God and for His glory in the nation. Be a vessel. Enlarge your tent – greater than you imagine. Hold steady at times of testing. God will finish what he has established.
>
> He will not lead you where He does not feed you. He will not guide you where He will not provide. Continue to walk in obedience.

What a word and as we look to the next couple of months and 1998 I sense the word, Ecclesiastes 11:4: "Whoever watches the wind will not plant; whoever looks at the clouds will not reap."

If I looked to the circumstances, I would just sit tight and wait until some money comes in and then move. If I had waited for the circumstances to change and become favourable I would never have started CAP. If I had felt that circumstances reflected what God thought of our ministry and myself I would have packed in many times. Praise God for His word and His encouragement through brothers and sisters. I am taking tomorrow off to spend the day away from work. I have lots and lots to do but it will all wait and I sense it is a time of reflection at the end of a truly amazing year. The next four weeks are crucial in the run up to Christmas, very busy and with lots of decisions to make. Our prayer letter went out today along with 60 videos of clients saying thank you to everybody who has supported our ministry. Malcolm West has done a fantastic job making our video – giving his time and talent free of charge. I pray people will respond to our work but I am beginning to see that it is not by my might or in my power but by His spirit. I pray people will be moved to support us in prayer and in practical finance and I just know that God will provide the £100,000 we will need next year. I know this because I know we are in His will, doing His work and He "Knows the end from the beginning" and is not altered from His goal by man and his reactions to events. Praise GOD!

Here we see in a very simple way just how we started to press forward when we didn't have the funding; from this point on, up to and including May 2003. We have never had the money to pay for any new position we have ever offered. We have simply decided that God wanted us to do it and we have gone ahead. Every single person who has ever worked for us, over 75 in total, including the 61 existing staff have all joined us knowing we didn't have the funding to pay our existing team. However, they have all stepped out in faith and that faith has been vindicated. We have never not paid any staff wages; yes they have been 'a little' late (up to two months) but God has honoured every contract of employment we have ever given out.

We have a great system of paying staff. Every month the staff that have pressing needs, the ones who are the only wage earners within a family, are given preference by other staff and get paid first. Then the rest wait in faith for their money. We have never allowed anybody to get more than two months behind everybody else. It's an amazing ongoing testimony to God working in a way that would seem ridiculous to us, yet that is the way He has decided to grow this ministry.

We have only been completely up-to-date about twice but God has been faithful and as I write this on May 31, 2003, at the end of year seven, we were only £50,000 short of being completely up to date. This represents just about two weeks costs and over the seven years we had received just over £2.5 million pounds. The £50,000 short represented just 2% of our total income. In other words, God had provided 98% of our needs. I have no doubt He will eventually bring us up-to-date, as regular income increases. So that, as a percentage of our needs, the pressure will continue to reduce. However, I never want us to become a budget-driven ministry that decides what to do based on what resources it has. We will always need to have faith mixed with wisdom.

The next five months to our financial year end in May were as eventful as ever and we were basically beginning to devise the systems and procedures that would allow us to start expanding the work with our first centre opening in September 1998. Many of the services we use today such as budget accounts, insolvency etc. were established in this very important period. Our confidence that God was with us continued to grow as did our supporters.

December 16, 1997

As we approach Christmas, I can feel the pressure increasing not only for myself but also for the charity. We have just ordered the fourth computer which we need and after paying all the bills due for the end of December, we have nothing left. I just know that God will provide for our needs of £4,000 in January.

What seems strange is that it's our personal financial situation which causes me more concern than anything. After we get my wage and we have paid all our bills and tithes we have very little left for the next four weeks including Christmas. I became depressed last night and seemed unable to shake off the feeling of isolation and depression over our financial situation. Don't get me wrong. I know that we are blessed, but the relentless pressure of lack of money just wears me down.

Why do we have to suffer like this I ask myself, and no sooner have I written the words then I am convicted of just how much God has provided and will provide in the future. God's big enough for my failings and my disappointment with our situation. He knows how I feel anyway, it is not a 'news flash' to Him that I'm struggling and He sympathises with our needs and pains. Our desperate situation has again motivated me to build CAP, through the Lord, to help other people who are in my position but without our knowledge and faith in God. How do people get through life without God on their side?

Again I have had to deal with thoughts of how people continue not to respond to both our needs and those of the charity. I know people base their decisions on what they see. When will people get a hold of God's heart towards giving and supporting each other? I believe that when that day comes we will see revival through people's pockets – an area that seems last to be affected by God's spirit of generosity and love.

I know there are thousands of people who give huge amounts sacrificially to the Lord's work. I decided to leave it in just to show how I was feeling. I praise God that this never established a root of bitterness or resentment within me, it could have so easily.

December 27, 1997

I am struck by just how far we've come with God's help. Last year at this time I was on my own and had just begun CAP. Over

the year we have proved beyond any doubt that, with God's
help, we can make a real difference in people's lives. Letter
after letter from people tell me that we are changing their lives.
We know that our work is being used by God to set the
captives free and people are getting saved.

We have also learned that not everyone takes up our offer of
help. We have been disappointed and have been let down by
our clients along the way. The secret must be to use the very
precious and limited resources at our disposal to best effect. We
have no alternative but to move on if clients we help are not
responding. You can lead a horse to water but you can't make it
drink. Because we are looking for sustainable poverty relief we
have to empower clients to trust us and change how they live. If
they refuse to work with us there is nothing we can do. We
need to concentrate on the people we can help and who will
work with us. We need to have the confidence in God's ability
to bring people back to us if they don't respond first time
around. Until then, we have to let them go.

This is a fact that we are still having to deal with today and it's
very hard and can so easily be misunderstood. Imagine you are a
caseworker trained in debt counselling with amazing budgeting
and debt repayment services at your fingertips. You know that if
a couple will just work with you, live within their means, agree
and pay into a budget account and co-operate, that their lives will
be transformed. Yet they just won't work with you, there may be
children going hungry, their home may be about to be repossessed
and there is nothing you can do.

We put a lot of effort into training and supporting particularly
new caseworkers to deal with this side of our work. On a positive
note we have seen many clients come back to us and we will
always give people another chance if they are truly sorry and want

to try again. It just gets harder as creditors become more sceptical each time our clients don't stick to repayment schedules.

December 27, 1997 continued

What does 1998 hold for us all? It is the most exciting, challenging and frightening thing I have ever faced. There will be four of us by February with a monthly budget of approximately £8,000. We are £78,000 short of our needs for the whole year and we need £4,000 in January alone. The new staff will need to be trained and the whole dynamics of the ministry will change, expansion is inevitable and my responsibilities will continue to increase and expand.

We still have great difficulties with our financial situation of a large mortgage and basically insufficient money to meet our needs every month from my salary. But God is so good we never want for anything. At the moment we have just £50 to last us four weeks but my faith continues to increase in line with our needs. What will happen with our house and mortgage? Who knows. All I know is that God will do whatever needs to be done to provide for our needs of somewhere to live and the ability to meet our commitments, pay our bills and be blessed with abundant provision. That's the heart of my God. He's not stingy. He does not withhold without reason and that can only be for our good in the long term. What a joy it is to just know that you are in God's hands and He takes away the responsibility and pressure. Praise God for that indescribable gift of peace.

February 6, 1998

Caroline Bateman joined us in January as a part-time help with admin and fund-raising. With Ruth now with us the sense of elation at seeing four of us working for CAP is almost impossible to describe. What a resource from God to us for His work in the city.

Caroline Bateman, William Spencer, myself, Ruth Barber (née Graves)
(Photograph reproduced by kind permission of the Telegraph and Argus, Bradford)

What a wonderful weekend it has been. I was paid £150 from CAP. This meant we could afford to go away and buy Lizzie some boots that she needed. Then over the weekend we received £125 as a gift and right at the end the promise of £250 in a couple of weeks. Then yesterday another gift of £100 came from a brother down in Aldershot. The result of all this is that we have survived another two weeks, have enough for food for the next week and yet again God has broken through with His provision.

As far as the charity is concerned, we still need £1,000 this month and £6,000 next month but I just know it will come in. Although I wish we had the money on hand it's obviously not God's way at the moment. However, I sense that soon, very soon, we are going to be blessed and have some in the store house.

The following diary section describes one of the first times we saw God dramatically intervene in a case with CAP. There is always a future hope, always a way forward and with God on our side we need not be fearful of any solicitors or judges or bailiffs. The couple concerned encapsulate the whole work we undertake. It was cases like this, week in week out, that were and remain today our great motivation. I pray you get a sense of what we do and how we work with families to release them from indescribable difficulties.

February 15, 1998

Yesterday I got a phone call from a next-door neighbour of an elderly couple who were in a desperate situation. I went round straight away. Something told me this was a vital one and it required me now. When I got there they were in a desperate state, they were to be evicted at 10.30am, Monday. The husband had been told he needed to go into a local psychiatric hospital and he said he would go on Monday if he lost the house.

His wife was suffering from shock. She had been confused and had hidden from him their true financial situation. It was only when the bailiffs called at her house on the Friday and told her to get all the furniture out that she realised what things had come to. The bailiff, as many are, was reasonable and could see she hadn't even packed. He actually drove her to court to have the repossession notice suspended until 10.30am Monday and told the locksmith to go away. Apparently the locksmith was not very happy. I spent about an hour trying to calm them down and get enough information to mount a challenge to the repossession order at court on Monday at 10.15am and I felt a tremendous sense of love and compassion for this couple.

If ever I needed confirmation that I was in the right place and in God's will it was being with this couple. They had nothing and nobody else to help them, they were in shock and unable to comprehend what was happening. They had nowhere to go or to live and were decent elderly people who had fallen on hard times and did not know what to do. I need to appear with them in court on Monday and to try to get the repossession suspended and then try and resolve the difficulties which I know, given a couple of months, I can do.

One of the scriptures which comes to mind is Proverbs 22:22–23 which is one of our principle inspirations. It says "Do not exploit the poor because they are poor and do not crush the needy in court, for the Lord will take up their case and will plunder those who plunder them".

Praise God that He has taken up their case and He will be with me in court on Monday. He is much bigger than the judge and the landlord's solicitors. I just need to rest in His word and have faith that He will come to the rescue of this couple. This situation is exactly what our ministry is based upon, Proverbs 31:8–9 "Speak up for those who cannot speak for themselves, for the rights of all who are destitute. Speak up and judge fairly; defend the rights of the poor and needy."

Psalm 10:17–18: "You hear, O Lord, the desire of the afflicted; you encourage them, and you listen to their cry, defending the fatherless and the oppressed, in order that man, who is of the earth, may terrify no more". I know that God will be true to His word and I pray that we win the court case on Monday and keep this lovely couple in their home where they have been for the last 13 years.

February 16, 1998

What a day!

Appeared at court at 10.25am and God miraculously intervened. After several minutes of the landlord's solicitor ranting on and on about how hopeless my client had been the county court judge told her: "Be quiet!" She just shut up. It gave me chance to explain the case and ask for leniency. The judge gave me a 30-day suspension order, and so I had to run across the courthouse to get to the bailiff's office before they set off at 10.30. I arrived at 10.29, just in time to hand the bailiffs the suspension order.

God is good and what a witness and motivation to everyone associated with CAP! Without our being there and available to help, this couple would have been dumped out on the street with nothing and nowhere to live.

Just to update you with this couple, they became model clients, they paid all their debts off including £1,500 rent arrears, cleared all their other credit and started saving. They moved into sheltered accommodation and were still working with us when in May 2002 they both prayed a prayer of salvation. Shortly after the lady died. However, her husband now attends a local church and is doing well.

Over the years we have appeared in court hundreds of times to get reposession orders suspended. Time and time again providing there is a good enough chance of things being worked out, we have had amazing judgements given to us by sympathetic judges. Literally hundreds of families have followed in the footsteps of this first case and almost every week we hear a testimony of similar supernatural events that save peoples' homes and keep families together.

February 25, 1998

I had to use £14 I had put on one side for my daughter's birthday present. However we got through and God did provide for our food, not exactly as I would have expected. We often want to have enough money for the next few days, the next week or the next month or year but in the wilderness God provided daily.

Over the last couple of days God has poured out His provision. Three people gave us £50 and when I paid all the bills out I didn't have to pay the Council tax for two months which meant I had over £100 left out of my wage. This is amazing and although it doesn't sound a lot it's more than the £3.77 I had left last month.

All the staff got paid their wages and again God provided just when we needed it. We were several hundred pounds off paying everyone but we stepped out in faith and wrote the cheques and split one salary into two to give God a couple more days. We needn't have bothered, three gifts of £400, which normally take up to four weeks to clear through the banking system, cleared at 10.30am, 14 days earlier than normal and guess what our shortfall was? Yes, just under £400. God is so good and provides in so many ways.

This next entry reminds me that even in the midst of God's provision we ourselves can still fall way short. I know Lizzie has had to put up with me many times over the years. But reading what she put up with as a sacrifice for the ministry I am convicted of my own actions. I am so grateful, she continually forgives me for my lack of grace. She is a wonderful woman of God who has faithfully been by my side through thick and thin.

March 17, 1998

I have been so insecure and emotional during the weekend. I got very irritable with Lizzie and went into a self-pity party. We were also very tight for food-shopping money. However, the Lord brought me through and I know that many are praying for us and we will get through – but it's tough.

It's times like this when we have nothing and I can't provide for my family's basic needs that I feel a little let down. God knows my heart and it won't always be like this. He will reward us for our trials and sufferings as the word says:

> Consider it pure joy, my brothers, whenever you face trials of many kinds, because you know that the testing of your faith develops perseverance. Perseverance must finish its work so that you may be mature and complete, not lacking anything.
>
> (James 1:2–4)

March 23, 1998

A great weekend, even though our personal circumstances were dire. Lizzie had an uncomfortable supermarket experience and had to put food back at the check out. We actually reached less than £1 between us and the great sense of God was wonderful. By His Holy Spirit we were able to praise God in a wonderful way, we had tremendous praise and worship over the weekend. We just knew that God would turn up something for us. Then first thing this morning I came down to an envelope, which someone had put through our letterbox, and in it was £250 pounds with no indication of who had given it. What an awesome God we have! I could pay what I owed, we gave our tithe and another gift and we still had enough for next week's food.

I pray the person who put this money through our letterbox will read this and know just how they provided for us. Also, for anyone who has ever given any financial support to anyone without them knowing who gave it, I pray you are encouraged to carry on. To anyone who has never done such a thing "Now is the Time" says the Lord!

Matthew 6:3–4: "but when you give to the needy, do not let your left hand know what your right hand is doing, so that your giving may be in secret. Then your Father, who sees what is done in secret, will reward you."

CAP operates like this. Whenever we give any financial support for food for CAP clients we make sure they know it's come through CAP not anyone in particular. They never know who has actually given us the money to make it possible. That way God gets the glory and everyone who has ever given to CAP gets the reward.

March 23, 1998 continued

God is so good and faithful. I still don't understand why He waited until this morning. Perhaps He just wanted to see if our praise and worship was based on our circumstances and feelings or on our unconditional love for God. What an honour that through His Holy Spirit we may have begun to learn how to praise Him in spirit and truth rather than because life is easy for us on that day.

March 25, 1998

Well, wages day has come and we are still several thousand pounds short. However, we have got £1,500 and we know that £5,500 will come in over the next week. Therefore we have all had to sit down and work out what we all need to pay our various standing orders for the next week. We are going to

divide what we have according to each person's needs. What a
wonderful example of God's people working together: Ruth and
Caroline say they can get by for another week which means that
both William and I can just clear our standing orders for
mortgage and other essential payments. Whoever said being a
Christian was boring? It's the most challenging and exhilarating
thing I could ever imagine.

This was just one example of the many times staff have favoured
each other when wages are due. Still to this day we share out the
wages we have. Now the salary bill is over £55,000 a month and
we have 61 staff. However, the foundations laid in the early days
by the four of us have been very strong and it remains a testimony
to God's people preferring each other, putting the needs of others
before their own. Praise God.

March 25, 1998 continued

We are holding our monthly staff meeting and reviews today
and all our talk will be on the future expansion and ongoing
work of our ministry. Can you imagine in the outside world in a
normal business run under any accepted accountancy or
business a boss sitting down with staff and telling them to pray
for their wages? Then asking them to decide who should get
what little money you have got. Then start talking about
expanding the business and taking on more staff. Are we mad? It
is only the grace of God working in our lives that could give us
the fruit that we have seen over the last few weeks. What a gift
to be content and have a spirit of praise and worship that is
unaffected by the circumstances that surround us!

10.30am same day

After we checked the bank account we were still short. Some
money that was expected did not come in. Then the post

arrived. Now we have two cheques for £500 – both from totally unexpected sources. This means that we can all cover our needs this weekend for standing orders for our mortgages etc. Then when the £5,500 comes in next week we can all be paid and our outstanding bills will be cleared. Praise God for His faithfulness and for His provision and I get a sense that He is not finished yet and that we might be overwhelmed before the end of the week.

May 6, 1998

What a weekend we had! The most wonderful conference at church and it was wonderful to see God's presence and all that went on. Over the weekend we got a letter from the Rank Benevolent Memorial Trust saying they would give us £23,500 over the next three years: £10,000 now and the rest spread over the next two years. God is so good and this gives us some breathing space over the next few weeks and means that our accounts will be in wonderful shape when we finish our financial year-end at the end of this month.

May 31, 1998

We have just finished our second year and what a year it was. Our income has grown almost eight-fold. With more than 160 people helped, and three full time and one part time staff, it's almost impossible to imagine that this time last year I was still on my own, with William just volunteering one day a week. It has been a miracle to see how God has touched our lives and blessed the work of CAP. Although looking back I can see just how hard it has all been, in places.

Our results at the end of our second year were again astonishing. We had helped 167 individual clients and our income had gone up from £10,413 in the first year to an amazing £84,796. That's an eight-fold increase on the previous year. We had established the basic systems for doing what we did, we had proved that I could train other people to do the debt counselling, and more and more people are becoming Christians! What an amazing second year and I believe that it was the year the foundations were laid for the way CAP changes lives.

CHAPTER SEVEN

GOD SPEAKS: "DON'T HOLD BACK" AND CAP's CHURCH CENTRES START OPENING

All the time the work was expanding, more and more families were being helped, many were getting saved and being added to the church. We were more settled than we had been for two years. Did we pause and catch our breath? I don't think so.

I had always known that the misery of debt we were seeing was not particular to Bradford. I knew that if we were to really begin to make an impact on such a huge nationwide problem we had to find a way to expand the operation without losing the ingredients that made us distinctively church based and evangelistic.

I began to look at the make-up of CAP and what had made us so successful in Bradford. There were four vital things. Firstly we had one church, Christian Life Church and a leader, Paul Hubbard, who really believed in our work and was able to transmit that enthusiasm to his congregation. Secondly we needed a person who was willing to join CAP and be trained as a debt counsellor. This person would be the one who would pioneer the work in the church and the town. We also needed faith that God would provide which had to be shared by both the church and CAP. Finally we needed a training and support system based in Bradford to support and keep up the momentum at remote centres.

It's very interesting that in the past I had been involved in expanding consumer finance companies by opening centres in new towns. I now see how this experience and knowledge of how to create basically a 'franchised' workable system was a very effective way of duplicating and growing any successful business. I also saw how it was to help launch CAP into the next and most demanding phase.

We had a great relationship with Kings Church, Aldershot, and Derek Brown the pastor had invited me to share the vision. I had already helped a couple of the congregation who were struggling with debt issues. Obviously through this Derek saw something he was willing to embrace and pioneer. Aldershot was to become the first remote centre which opened in September 1998.

At this time I knew so little about what I was about to do but somehow just felt that this was the only way that would allow rapid expansion of our work over the coming years.

Year three June 1998 to May 1999

During the summer we went full steam ahead preparing for the opening of our very first CAP centre in Aldershot. We were beginning to develop the strategy of opening centres. It was a ridiculous thing to do bearing in mind our ongoing needs. Even looking back six years I am stunned by the 'lets just do it' mentality and faith in what we did. It remains today another expression of the faith that has been the backbone of CAP for the last six years. Today, we still decide to expand without the money. Never have we had the wages to be able to pay all the existing staff when we have stepped out in faith and taken on more people.

There was by now a relentless pace of moving forward in what

God had called us to. As the summer progressed things started to move quite quickly, even by our standards.

August 1, 1998

What a last two months that's been, so much has happened at such a pace.

There was the first CAP newspaper which we did over the last eight weeks. It was an incredible venture inspired by God which took weeks and weeks to complete. We had 26 articles to write, and we also had to learn how to write articles.

Lizzie has just lost her mum and although in some ways it was blessing for her to have no more pain it has been a very difficult time for Lizzie and her family. She carries so much so well and I don't really appreciate her as I know I should.

We have also moved forward with the vision of a national network of centres with the opening of our first centre in Aldershot. God has brought Peter and Avril Wood to head up our office in Aldershot. Again this has been led by God and although there have been some teething problems, we are going ahead again in faith that it's right in God and He will provide for us.

It has to be said that Aldershot Centre has in many ways been one of the most important centres to CAP. Yes, we have had difficulties and I have sometimes thought the centre would close. But time and time again the Lord has kept things going forward. Aldershot is still open and over five years has seen over 250 clients and last year saw eight peopled saved. The church continues to support the ministry and remains one of the most generous in terms of financial support.

August 1, 1998 continued

I am again struggling with people's lack of support to our work. How can it be that we write to over 250 known Christians and get just three responses? One more regular giver and three small donations from people I don't really know. I wonder if God will ever reveal to me what it is about regular financial support that is so difficult. If 50 people just gave £1 per week although in real terms the amounts would be small what a joy to know that another fifty people are willing to step out and support our work. It's almost as if people are turned off by something we do. Are we too challenging, professional, adventurous? Is it jealousy or simply that people are tight with their finances and refuse to give to our cause? I need God to give me a perspective on how people look at us and the work we do. Then again perhaps it best not to know and concentrate on what God thinks about our work. As I said recently, God does not change His mind because of what other people think.

Here was this ongoing difficulty with what we perceived as a lack of support. As you can see I really did struggle with this one. If I'm honest I still do in a much smaller way than back in 1998. I left this entry in as I always think there is no point saying everything is rosy when you are struggling. I have to say I'm so glad we never gave up on regular givers. They were to become known as "life changers". In the last six months alone we have received just over 400 "life changers" which is 16 times the number I generated in the first two years!! I pray every one of them is encouraged by just how much their support has meant to us over the years. If you are not a "life changer" just fill in the form at the back, cut it out and – most importantly – send it to us now! Don't put it off! We need your support and encouragement. If we are to grow and touch even more lives and open even more centres we need you to join us and we would love to have you with us in this amazing journey.

September 19, 1998

Aldershot is now open and although I was a little disappointed by how one member the leadership team has dealt with us, I sense God saying to me "now you know how I feel when you don't live up to My expectations. However, I still use you and love you despite your actions". I know that over the next thirty years I will have to deal with many churches and people who disappoint me and who I disappoint. However, by God's grace we will complete the calling and CAP will play its part in changing a nation through hundreds of imperfect churches and thousands of imperfect people just like me.

It's very interesting to see how, even in those early days, I was sensing that God was teaching me many things. I obviously had an expectancy that the work would grow. I'm not sure about the hundreds of churches. We have our hands full working with the thirty now.

September 19, 1998, continued

Liverpool, Huddersfield, Worcester and South West Nottingham are also beginning to open up, its so exciting to see God's plans and purposes coming together. I could never have foreseen what joy I feel to play my part in His great commission. Let's see how God works out the next month. It's going to be another testimony of His faithfulness and provision.

No money as yet, things just seem to get tighter and tighter. We have to use money that is set aside for other things to pay for food-shopping and I have even had to consider using the Visa

card that came in today. Maybe God is telling me that I have to
have the faith to use my Visa card in the same way that I know
He will provide for me to pay it off. We still need £6,000 to be
able to pay the wages next week and I have absolutely no idea
where the money is to come from.

This week I got the following word

> "Enlarge the place of your tent, stretch your tent curtains
> wide, do not hold back; lengthen your cords, strengthen your
> stakes. For you will spread out to the right and to the left; your
> descendants will dispossess nations and settle in their desolate
> cities. Do not be afraid; you will not suffer shame. Do not fear
> disgrace; you will not be humiliated."
>
> Isaiah 54:2–4

I feel this speaks directly to me about strengthening my
foundations, just opening up and spreading out. It also says that
we will not suffer shame and that we will not be humiliated.
I know that God will not let us down as we step out in faith to
pay people properly and expand our work. My prayer is quickly
Lord, quickly Lord.

This was the first time I was drawn to Isaiah 54:2–4. It was just
one of those times when seeking God and reading His word that
you feel in your spirit that God Himself wrote these words for you.
Over the years it has become one of our most important scriptures
and has been a real encouragement to press ahead. It's framed in
my office and virtually every day I read it and meditate on God's
promises in these few short verses.

Each time we have opened centres we have not had the money
to pay even the first month's wages. It's as if we are tested at each
point of expansion. Each time we have said "nevertheless, let's
press forward". I particularly like v4, which says "Do not be afraid;

you will not suffer shame. Do not fear disgrace; you will not be humiliated."

I realise now this shame and humiliation is in the Lord's eyes, not in the hearts or words of men and women. Many times I have suffered shame before man and been humiliated by our lack. However, I know that the Lord has never been ashamed or humiliated by what we do and I believe there is great honour when you suffer at the hands of men for a godly inspired vision.

October 5, 1998

Well, God was true to His word and we did get paid. Eventually a series of miracles happened. One – a client – who had sold his house to clear his debts and make a fresh start called and to our astonishment said he wanted to sow £2,000 into the ministry. Second, one of the couples who came to see us about setting up Nottingham sent £1,000 from their church's trust fund. Several Trusts sent a few hundred pounds. We have just paid all our bills and still have about £1,500 for this month only £6,000 to go. It's incredible to look back and see just how faithful God is.

We have just had a Trustees meeting where our plans to open ten new centres have just been approved. This means that by the middle of next year, May 1999, we will have ten centres reaching out into their communities.

On a less positive note we were forced to use a small overdraft from the bank to pay everybody we owed money to, which now means we need about £2,000 to get everything paid off. Only God knows how this will all work out. I am going to America on Thursday to raise money for the charity and a building we are trying to get with our church.

This was a crucial point for CAP. Did we step out and hire the staff or did we hold back? I still can't quite believe we actually sent out the job offers and contracts. There is always a point where there is no going back; where you become totally reliant on God, when you go beyond your own and anyone else's understanding or rational thoughts. This was that point of no return, from this point the bridges were well and truly burnt.

There have been many times just like this and it continues today but there will never be another first time you lay down a principle, a foundation. I praise God for the faith and boldness He gave the staff and the trustees to support me at that time.

October 21, 1998

As the weeks have progressed the financial situation got more desperate. Here I am, wanting to take on three new staff when I am about £5,000 short of paying the wages of the ones I already have. By Friday nothing had come in and I was faced with the decision about sending out the job offers to the new staff. I felt deep down that it was right to go for it. I felt God saying: "If it's right, act as if you have the money and send out the job offers". I sent them out and waited to see where the money to pay us all would come from. Saturday's post came and went. Nothing, no money. Nevertheless I just carried on with the weekend and thought very little about our predicament.

October 25, 1998

It is my birthday and unbeknown to me, Lizzie and the staff had pulled out all the hand written mail for me over the week thinking they were birthday cards. As I opened one, out fell a cheque for £6,000, from the man I had spoken to earlier in the week. From his letter it appears that he suffered great financial hardship in the 80s and longed for some practical help like CAP offers. He said he wanted to bless our work with some of the immeasurable blessing God had given him.

> The letter came into the office on Thursday morning so when I sent the job offers out the cheque was only a few inches away from me but I didn't know. God just wanted to know whether my decision was based on what I could see in terms of finance and what I knew to be the right thing to do.
>
> Praise God for His faithfulness.

I pray the couple who sent this cheque read this and understand the significance of their gift. Re-reading the diary entry I am taken aback yet again that the cheque was a few inches away from me when I sent out the job offers and contracts. God is amazing and through these events the faith of people around me and my own began to increase. It's through these early events that God obviously began moulding the ministry into the faith-filled, faith-directed, God-focused work of today!

November 27, 1998

> Just one month since that fantastic miracle of £6,000 in my drawer here we go again.
>
> We even had to divide up what money we had amongst the staff this week and it is always a very humbling thing to see staff preferring each other in terms of paying salaries. Nothing came in until the last phone call at 5.45pm on Friday from Tear Fund saying they had agreed another grant for £10,000. We would get this within the next ten days. I wonder if they really know just how vital their encouragement is to us on the front line. Anyway this meant that even if we had to borrow, we could all get paid the next week. I somehow got a sense that God hadn't finished yet.
>
> Here again we see Tear Fund's support just in time. I hope David Evans, who helped with these first few years' support, understands just what it meant to us.

November 27, 1998 continued

On Sunday a couple from our church gave us £323 and after William had added in the regular income we could expect over the next few days we were just £1,000 short. Then, on Monday, at about 11am a pastor and amazing man of God from a local church, called in unexpectedly. We had added a couple of our clients to his congregation. He just gave us a cheque for £500 from the church and £500 from himself. I was totally taken aback by the generosity of this church and this pastor. It was as if an angel had walked among us. We finished the month with £150 to spare and knowing we would get paid in December only the second month in two years that we had the wages at the beginning of the month. Praise God for His provision.

These were very special times and many of these people continue to support CAP now. Everybody who has ever sent any money needs to know just how vital they have been to what we do.

January 18, 1999

Things are really starting to hot up. We are now on the threshold of a new year and I can't quite imagine what it holds in store. By the end of the month there will be 14 people working for CAP. Our monthly needs in terms of salaries etc will have risen to £14,000. A huge amount when you consider that we only have about £2,000 per month in regular income. We really need about £6,000 this month to pay the NI and tax bill for December and January and then £12,000 in February.

I don't know if it's fear, the flesh or God but I really sense that we need to move up a gear in terms of income. Trust income seems to be slowing down with fewer repeat donations and no real new ones to go for. What should I do and why does finance play such a huge part in my thinking now? God knows what we need and I am certain all the finance will come in but will it always be hand-to-mouth? We need to be honourable in our finances and pay people and NI and tax on time. Will God bring someone who pours some real finance into us soon or will we get the money on the drip each and every month. This is now the 23rd out of 25 months when we started the month without enough money to pay the wages for the month.

The national lottery charities board application is held up in red tape with the matter of our employment policy of only employing Christians. Who knows what they will say, and even then I have a massive four-year business plan to write.

The insolvency work with clients is really getting going yet straight away we are running into problems with finance companies refusing to help us. We have a huge amount of work to do to make the service work. It will take time and effort to drive it forward.

Matt and Josie Barlow are coming to Bradford this weekend and are joining us from February the 1st. What a joy it will be when they join us and increase the resources here in Bradford by 40%.

The joining of Matt and Josie was very much a key event in the life and history of this ministry. They moved from Cheltenham, gave up two good jobs and made a major commitment to the ministry. They continue to be very close both as friends and as work colleagues. Matt is now the Operations Director running the whole centre network and the support departments that numbers about 40 staff. He has played a huge role in developing the whole operational work of CAP, a great effective manager with wisdom and discernment.

Josie is funding and PR manager and over the last four years she has been with us she has totally transformed our funding strategy and now leads a team of three who look after a budgeted income of over £1,200,000. They are an amazing couple who have done so much for CAP.

They are the type of people who will see when I am struggling and have a way of lifting me and supporting me through some very difficult times. They are full of faith and both have the amazing and rare ability to make things happen around them.

They both have made such a difference in how CAP has grown and they have both laid down a foundation upon which the Lord will build for many years and generations to come.

Matt Barlow writes . . .

Since giving myself to Jesus in 1992 (six weeks before John), God has given me two passions. One is to care for the poor and needy and the other is to lead people to know God and have their lives transformed. Two years spent in the Dominican Republic gave me great experience at doing these things but I was sure that there must be some way of doing the same in the UK.

You can imagine how excited I was when this bloke from Yorkshire came to speak at our church in Cheltenham. So off I set on a mission to open my own CAP centre; little did I know!

Within hours of being with John, after he had barely got to know me and even less of Josie, he was offering us both jobs. We weren't aware that the previous week John and Paul had prayed and asked God for two people, Someone to help run centres and someone to work in fundraising (Josie had been training in fundraising over the previous year). We prayed like mad and felt God speak to us in a number of ways. Josie then visited Bradford and within six weeks we had given up our jobs, given notice on our flat and moved to Bradford.

Since that time both Josie and I have had the awesome privilege of being at John and Lizzie's side and serving both them and God to see many people released from oppression and many come to know Jesus through the work of CAP.

It has been a challenging time in many, many ways but also an amazing time of God taking the gifts that He had given us in the first place and using them way beyond anything we thought we would ever achieve.

We have seen the power of encouragement, the power of belief in others and just trusting them and letting them just "have a go". We have seen the need to be well organised, practical and strategic while constantly being open to God and allowing Him to do things how ever He wants.

Every testimony that comes in of mums having money to buy food and talking of the 'luxury' of having £50 per week for food bowls me over. People talk of the amazing feeling of being able to buy Christmas presents with their own money. Perhaps one of the biggest ones for me is the husbands and wives who are still together as a result of our work.

Above all else, the reason we do what we do is to help people discover Jesus. God has told me we are evangelists who do debt counselling, not debt counsellors who do evangelism. To see the smiles and the tears and the transformed lives make absolutely every difficulty and every challenge worth it.

Matt Barlow, Operations Director.

By now in early 1999, Lizzie was seven months pregnant and our house had been converted to four offices with seven to ten people working in the house every day! We needed a home, somewhere Lizzie could have her first child and we could be separated from the work for our sanity. As you will see, yet again, God did provide for us just in time.

January 18, 1999 continued

Our house needs are still causing me great concern. A Christian brother has said that he will buy us a house and we can then rent it from him at a reduced amount. He would then let us buy the house from him when we can. There is little hope of us getting a mortgage for about two years. The only problem is that he never seems to phone me with an answer to anything and I am beginning to doubt if he is serious. It must be God who is driving this thing forward. Lizzie is now seven months pregnant; we need somewhere to live soon and we have no resources other than God. I pray that God will move soon and find us a house. We feel a bit under pressure.

I also sense that people are beginning to say that we have grown too big, too soon as a charity and we should draw back. Even the prayer team's notes seemed to suggest we might be off track and that I needed to be more holy etc. I know all this but I still feel we are exactly where God wants us to be and within His ability to steer us forward. I have got my great brother in Paul (Hubbard) who I know would shout if he felt I was going off track. I know that despite what other people may think, we are right to step out in complete faith in God. As the word says it is IMPOSSIBLE to please God without faith. I am certain that He will provide for all our needs and that He has grown CAP – not me – and where He leads, He feeds. I know that God will carry on with His faithful support of our ministry.

February 20, 1999

A good month as far as the charity work goes. We are moving forward on every front. With Matt and Josie starting we have got all departments moving forward. Bradford Centre continues to do well with Sue Forrest, Centre Manager, pushing the prayer and ministry team forward very well. Centre Operations and Insolvency teams are really starting to get going with Matt working very well alongside Ruth.

Fundraising has also moved forward with the completing of the 16-page, four-year development plan that is just being printed. Josie is now working with me on fundraising and I am confident that by June we will be in good shape.

Our problem remains the same as always – finance. We are now in debt owing two months' National Insurance (£5,000), need £7,000 to pay the wages due in five days as well as another £5,000 in bills etc. Never before have the figures been so big and there been nothing on the horizon. What can I say? That's how it is and God is big enough to handle my disappointment that yet again, we are down to a few days and the amounts are getting bigger.

Today I received a very hard letter from a brother who has a trust who could have given us a considerable gift. Not only did he not help us but wrote to me saying he felt we had grown too fast and that we were misguided in our plans and that I should ask God for clarity and go back to him with my amended plans.

People who have it within their power to help sometimes don't help and that's fine. It's when they say we are wrong as well, when it really hurts. Bless them for their honesty but I pray people with this sort of power would realise just how crushing their comments can be. These events continue to this day and I still find them hard. All I can do is recount the many who have resources and willingly give to our work.

February 20, 1999 continued

I actually wrote back to him and said that I had tried to understand his comments but that I was certain we were doing it God's way and that the work would go on irrespective of what others thought. I am stunned when people doubt whether we are in God's will. People are getting saved each month, the poor are being released from poverty and we are the ones paying the price through uncertainty. Everything we do we do for others. We are sold out to reach a nation and it is God who leads the way. I'm only responding to His call and His voice that has always said go forward. Still we wait to see if we are to get our new home and Lizzie is now seven-and-a-half months pregnant. We are now waiting for the building society to agree to us getting a mortgage then we need to find somewhere and complete and move-in, all in a few weeks.

Yet again it all seems surreal, here we are agreeing, in faith, to go on holiday in August when I don't have any food money after Thursday next week, have no house to move into and Lizzie is seven-and-a-half months pregnant.

We owe two months' tax and National Insurance which is hard to handle. However, I have just read Romans 13. It talks about submission to authorities and in verse 7 it says "Give everyone what you owe him; If you owe taxes, pay taxes, if revenue pay revenue; if respect, then respect; if honour, then honour."

I know that God will honour our commitment, meet our wages, needs and give us the ability to pay taxes. When and how are the only unknowns and who am I to second guess God? He can do what He wants but I know that it will ultimately be for our good.

Just to testify to God's provision we have eventually paid every tax and National Insurance due. Praise God!

February 20, 1999 continued

As I read back over the last few years it seems to be a cycle of great need and last minute provision, I wonder if this will always be the way. Will there ever be a day when we have a little spare? Will it always be last minute? Will every decision be in faith for his financial provision?

Nevertheless, only God knows and it's my duty to simply carry on regardless of circumstance and any doubts that people may share with me. God knows how I feel and what pressure Lizzie and I are under. He must be preparing us for something beyond our imagination because I never imagined that I would be faced with such difficulties, pressures, fears and lack of understanding when I started CAP nearly three years ago.

As I re-read this entry I can sense our acceptance of how God was leading us. I also sense gratitude for what He had given us. However, I still have a hope, that remains to this day, that one day the above will happen. I now see that the lack we have endured at times and the pressure we have withstood have very much been God's way of teaching us and testing us. It's been His way of laying some foundations in us upon which He can build.

May 21, 1999

What a wonderful three months we have had.

We did get a house, praise God! Elim church offered us their manse that is a four-bedroom detached house on the other side of Bradford. They only wanted one month's rent and even paid for us to decorate and carpet the house. Just in time. Lizzie was eight months pregnant when we moved into the new and beautiful house. God is so good and I will be eternally grateful in particular to Bob McDonald (Pastor of Elim Church) for his encouragement and help at this time.

The highlight was the birth of our daughter Abigail, born 13th April weighing 6lbs 9oz. What a wonderful month and the baby and Lizzie are doing so well. The birth was very traumatic with Lizzie having to have an emergency section after 15 hours of labour. Praise God for the medical services we have and God's hand of protection on our beloved daughter. It is times like this when everything is put into perspective; it's when you realise what's really important and just how much you have to praise God about.

Even in the midst of all this we had lots of problems with one particular church and two staff. It was a hard time but we all got through. My lack of maturity in terms of dealing with relationships with churches caused more problems. To a certain extent I sense that I was arrogant in my views and what I thought was right.

Paul Hubbard and I had to drop everything and with Abigail just eight days old we had to go and sort out the problems. It was a very difficult time. I felt the whole way we were called to do CAP was somehow being undermined. I now see that my insecurities, immaturity and lack of confidence all contributed to the problem. I was somehow fearful that we could lose all the ground we had gained over the last three years and that the way we had grown in faith and belief was being undermined. I think when you have put so much into something you can become terrified and very protective of it; wrong, but understandable.

May 21, 1999 continued

Again at a time of pressure and uncertainty God brought me back to Isaiah 54, v2–4 that I received back in September 1998 when we opened our first centre. God talks about spreading out, taking cities and then says: "Do not be afraid; you will not suffer shame. Do not fear disgrace; you will not be humiliated."

I am getting very close if not past the point of humiliation and shame, not paying wages, National Insurance, tax, outstanding invoices. In the natural I am afraid of not being able to pay wages. It makes me and the whole ministry look so bad. It's not right and I know that God should not allow it to come to pass that we are unable to pay our bills etc. but it happens. We will surely find out in the next two weeks just what the Lord can do. I just pray He will sell some of His cattle from some of His hills and send me the money soon.

This comes from Psalm 50:10 "For every animal of the forest is mine, and the cattle on a thousand hills."

May 31, 1999

The whole ministry continues to expand with 25 clients seen last month, almost as many as I saw in the whole first year. The team is growing here in Bradford to meet the challenge of the ever-increasing demands of the centre network.

Regular giving continues to grow and should reach approximately £3,500 in May, which is wonderful. Churches continue to give generously and I can see a bright future in terms of finance. It's just now that it feels very difficult.

Our year end was on the 31st of May and by some miracle we managed to pay all our outstanding bills except our wages for May. This has meant that the accounts show we actually balanced our books over the 12 months with an income of £157,460 and an expenditure of £161,366: a miracle in anyone's books.

As our third year drew to a close, as always somehow the money had just come in. We now had seven CAP centres (up from just one a year ago), had helped 329 people and seen our income grow from £84,796 to £157,460. We had seen many lives changed and many come to know the Lord. We had proved the principle of churches catching the vision and reaching out to the poor. What was the next year to hold for us? I somehow always knew it would be a rough ride and that our characters would be tested again and again.

We had seen great advances in what we did. We were beginning to get to grips with what it means to run remote centres and how to train, motivate and inspire people to follow a clearly defined vision. God had continued to be faithful and we were learning fast.

CHAPTER EIGHT

HARD TIMES

Year four June 1999 to May 2000

As we went into our fourth year, things really started to hot up. Our systems were starting to develop and things were speeding up in all areas of the ministry. We were about to enter our fifth year which was to see us grow by seven centres and increase everything by a third in just a year. We knew there were challenges ahead but we were in great spirits and expectant on what the Lord was about to do.

July 16, 1999

As always finance, or lack of it, continues to cause me the most difficulties. Today William, who manages the situation with great skill and under great pressure, showed me we needed approximately £30,000 to pay all our bills and the wages that are due over the next two weeks. We have only £3,000 in funds so to honour our commitments and bills we need £27,000 in two weeks!

Despite these worries, two other things are encouraging. The general response to our newspaper has been wonderful and on Wednesday we had a celebration evening with clients expressing in their own words just what it has meant to them to be helped by CAP. Lots of supporters came and it was a great night. It really lifted my spirits.

This next entry I feel shows just how desperate we had become and that I was on the verge of anger towards God for the continued situation. I am so pleased that over the years this occasional anger has been replaced with increasing calm and faith that God is in control and He knows why He is doing something. I now realise that He had a purpose in mind, which was to build our faith for what was to come over the next few years.

July 16, 1999 continued

When O God will you open up your storehouse and allow me to pay all my bills and wages on time? That is all I ask. Not for £150,000 in the bank (although not having to work as hard and commit as many resources to fund-raising and to be released from the grind of every increasing need would be wonderful). Only God knows. I just wish He would release the pressure and open up His storehouse door a little wider.

Who knows what the next few days and weeks over the summer will bring. The Lottery Fund decision will be made on Tuesday although we will not know for several weeks, that's £44,000 and would take the pressure off overnight.

Let's see how God will take us through the next few weeks.

I just want to explain our stance on applying for Lottery Fund money. I realise this is a controversial issue and many people have many different views. Firstly, I want to say that anyone or any organisation, church, charity etc. who decides on another way than ours, you have my complete support. Our decision was based on some simple things we felt were relevant to us.

We prayed and sought God. All the Trustees and management were involved in coming to the decision that we should at least apply. We realised that when we looked at the application procedure – a 70-page business plan and massive questioning of what we did – we realised that God could easily close the door if He did not want us to get the money. We were very careful that we did not in any way hide our objectives, one of which is "The advancement of the Christian faith". Nor did we conceal all the biblical reasons why we do what we do. We therefore applied in the January and asked for £225,000 over three years (This was only 20% of our expected needs).

July 29, 1999

Today, we got the wonderful news that the Lottery has decided to support our application with three year funding that amounts to £225,000. There is such joy in the place and the sense of relief is almost indescribable. You only realise just how much you need something when you actually get it.

There's lots to do before we get a penny and it will take several weeks before we receive any funds and we are still in great need at present with needs totalling over £20,000 and no idea where the funds will come from.

August 6, 1999

What a few days we have had! Our financial situation seems to get worse and worse. Yesterday William spoke to the Tax office about our overdue tax and National Insurance payments of just over £7,500. He was verbally threatened with county court action and a visit if we did not pay all our back National Insurance within a few days. We felt hurt at the aggressive way the tax office lady dealt with us. What a threat. God says in His Word we should pay our taxes and He will uphold His own commandment. Fear not.

August 6, 1999 continued

In the middle of all this, I was visited by a man from the local
Bishop's office regarding my complaint that for the second time
we had again not even been considered funding from the
Church Urban Fund. What a horrendous time. Absolutely no
encouragement, no flexibility and no recognition that our work
was good; just confirmation that we will not be supported. He
even said that if he personally had any money he would not give
us any!

The fund has rejected us because our clients are encouraged to
make very small donations back to our work. Also we are affecting
the whole nation by having a branch network that means we do
not affect local communities, apparently. In real terms we were
too small three years ago and now we are too big!

This was a difficult event for me to handle. This man made me
feel terrible. I wonder if he knew just how difficult and hurtful he
was, I honestly think he had no idea and I don't know which is
worst.

I have no doubt that funds from the Church Urban Fund are
released to good projects. However, I wanted you to know how
people engaged in difficult ventures suffer when they are rejected
for funding. You can say "no" to supporting someone in a way
that builds up, not pulls down.

This next entry covers a period of the worst financial need I
can recall, I nearly kept it out as it's so difficult to understand but
I wanted to include the triumphs and the difficult times. This
certainly shows both.

August 6, 1999 continued

Today I got a summary of our actual financial needs from William
before he goes away tonight and I have never faced such a

situation. We need £28,669.59 for all our bills and to pay the wages due, which are already two weeks late. We only have just over £100 in the Bank.

We have nothing on the horizon except a general promise from Empire Stores and Laing Trust. What can we do? It is just overwhelming and we are all feeling the pressure. This is a particularly difficult time, right in the middle of summer and holidays. We have nothing of ourselves left and there is real need among the staff.

We prayed and comforted each other. Perhaps God knew that we had to just take it today. We decided that there were only four things we had to do. First, Ruth phoned the bank but they refused an overdraft. The next call was to Paul (Paul Hubbard my Pastor). He already knew our situation and to his credit he managed to lend £3,000 of his own money just to pay one of the National Insurance bills. What a man of God!

I then called Derek Gardiner, a long time supporter of our work. Derek is a wonderful brother who runs a financial services company and I knew he would not be phased by our plight. I explained our situation and he said he would try to find someone to help us out. What another brother and man of God!

I am often asked why do we make our needs known to people and ask for help and how does that fit in with our faith. This is difficult to answer and I can only say that we have felt it right on occasions to ask for help and on others to say nothing. We also feel that it is good for people to give and by asking them you are encouraging them in the grace of giving. We are also asking for the whole charity needs rather than my own needs. I don't really know why it just sometimes feels right to ask and at other times just to wait on God.

August 6, 1999 continued

I have just taken a call from the Inland Revenue. The lady from before was on the other phone and the man I spoke to said he would pass the message on. He said that they might have to visit us to see how we were handling the charity and our obligations to tax and National Insurance. (Another threat!)

I can't believe that we have reached such an appalling state of affairs. We are virtually penniless with no ability to pay bills now due. We have no option but to stand in faith or simply lie down and almost die. That's how I feel. My flesh and body are completely at an end. There's almost a refreshing feeling to be so totally overwhelmed by a situation that you can do absolutely nothing about.

Many thoughts come into your mind at times like this. What did we do wrong? How can God allow us to suffer such shame and humiliation in His name's sake? What an appalling witness we are to the world, how could God allow this?

I have no answers, however one thing I know is that it's not over yet and all I can do is just stand and be strong trusting that my God will see us through.

It's at times like this when I find myself simply drawn to seek out what the Lord wants to say to me through His word. When I say the Lord has given me a certain word, I mean that through prayer and reading the bible I have felt deep down within me that this is what the Lord would want to say to me at any particular time. For me it's like He was sitting next to me and just talking to me, encouraging me and saying: "Keep going, son! Don't stop now. I am with you and will never forsake you." As you look at the appendix at the back of the book you will see just how well the Lord is able to encourage and inspire when we need it most.

August 6, 1999 continued

One verse that I have been meditating on today confirms this.

In Acts 5:41 it says: "The apostles left the Sanhedrin, rejoicing because they had been counted worthy of suffering disgrace for the Name" (of Jesus).

Even now I still stand on Isaiah 54:2–4a: ". . . Do not be afraid; you will not suffer shame. Do not fear disgrace; you will not be humiliated."

The overwhelming factual evidence that surrounds me says I am wrong, that I am in disgrace and humiliated. Somehow that does not affect the fact that deep down I know we are not humiliated in God's eyes and that He will get us through simply because He said He would.

October 8, 1999

What a two months that was. I really do not know how we managed to get through. The Lottery Fund eventually sent £14,000 towards the end of August and we have just struggled on from there. We reached new lows (or highs depending on how you look at things) when at the end of September none of the staff had been paid for two months. Every hope we had did not materialise. We were turned down by several Trusts and had to borrow money from our credit cards, not pay suppliers and juggle the money.

Last week reached a new crisis. We needed £35,000 to clear our bills and wages and had nothing coming in and we had reached the point of real hardship being experienced by staff and their families. Some were almost begging and borrowing to maintain mortgages, food, bills etc. How could this be allowed to go on? I felt dreadful and sick inside. What had I led people into? They trusted me and the vision yet where was God?

Every part of my flesh was screaming out you can't take any

more it's just too painful. Yet a still small voice said carry on and an even bigger voice inside my mind said I have no option what else can I do? I've come this far. I'm not stopping now.

I made a momentous decision to ring a close friend and ask if he would lend us £15,000. He agreed in such a gracious and encouraging way and although I knew this was getting serious I just had to do something. Several staff members and trustees felt very unhappy and to be honest we all struggled.

At a trustee meeting yesterday it was very difficult. The trustees were led by one person into fear and doubt about how we were funded and there were suggestions we should stop expanding and cut back on salaries. I felt so empty. Who apart from Paul would have said: "The work goes on whatever the circumstances"? Eventually we agreed to borrow the £15,000 next week to pay some wages and some suppliers but the pressure is never far away. Still £10,000 short of every bill and only two weeks before another £15,000 of wages and bills are due.

This next entry was and is a bit shocking to me as I re-read it. I know that it was all bound up with being challenged and tested by fear and man's thoughts. I also had on a daily basis client after client whose lives were being changed, people were getting saved throughout the country and we had long passed the point of no return. I was also surrounded by staff who believed, as I did, that we just had to carry on. What amazing people God had brought around me for such a test as what was about to befall us. The morale of the staff was very high, we all knew what we had joined and stood shoulder to shoulder and not for one minute did anyone say we should stop.

October 8, 1999 continued

> Someone said to me "what are you prepared to do to keep going?" The suggestion was that borrowing was a bridge too far. People don't understand just how far and to what lengths I am prepared to go and have gone to keep CAP afloat. If only people understood how much people need our help and the eternal value of our struggle to help people. They have no one to turn to. They are in such desperate situations.
>
> Another point of difficulty was when my pay was reviewed by the trustees when I left the meeting. What hurt me was that when I wasn't there they somehow managed to revert back to asking if they could afford a certain amount. There was no sense of faith, encouragement or support towards me. I felt that this was the only time in maybe a year that they needed to step out in faith for me and they didn't. In the end I resolved that my faith was in God. It is He who supports and encourages me. He is my provider not Trustees or the finances of the charity.

As it turned out it was one trustee who had basically argued very strongly about budgets. It was more a case that other trustees could not stand up to the logical and rational arguments. It was as if they were spectators to the work and faith we were showing. Each one in turn realised they needed to increase their own faith and belief in how we operated. This was a turning point in the charity. As it happened we were going to need this increased strength over the next few weeks and months. There was a challenge coming that they needed to be sharpened up for.

God is wonderful! Only He could use such an event to move the trustees to a new level of faith and determination and still today the trustees are a group of men and women of God who have their own faith and belief in what we do and will regularly step out in faith even more than I do.

October 21, 1999

The loan from my friend has caused a great deal of debate. Many simply felt it was not right. Others understood that I could do nothing else. It was as if God wanted to know whether other people had faith to repay a loan and that God can provide however He wants.

I felt desperate in the middle of all the pressure and had no real answer for anyone. I wondered who would press forward were I not here. I believe that there is only my Pastor Paul and a few very close employees like Matt, Josie, William, Caroline and Ruth, who really understand my heart. One person said "You would do anything even borrow money to keep this charity going". They said it in a quite critical way. If only they knew that I have already suffered and given up so much for this work of God and I would give everything up to keep it going.

As so often it is the word of God that gives me most comfort and encouragement to carry on.

"Here is my servant, whom I uphold, my chosen one in whom I delight; I will put my spirit on him and he will bring justice to the nations."   *(Isaiah 42:1)*

"I took you from the ends of the earth, from its farthest corners I called you. I said: "You are my servant; I have chosen you and have not rejected you. So do not fear, for I am with you; do not be dismayed, for I am your God. I will strengthen you and help you; I will uphold you with my righteous right hand."   *(Isaiah 41:9–10)*

"The poor and needy search for water, but there is none; their tongues are parched with thirst. But I the Lord will answer them; I, the God of Israel, will not forsake them. I will make rivers flow on barren heights, and springs within the valleys. I will turn the desert into pools of water, and the parched ground into springs."   *(Isaiah 41:17–18)*

October 22, 1999

> Yesterday I had, for the first time in a long time, some doubt
> about where we were going. Even after the loan and the other
> promised money, William showed me a list of bills and wages
> still to pay. I just felt low, as if there is no end to it all. I am
> interviewing three new staff, opening two new centres and
> pressing ahead in virtually all departments as if money was no
> object. The actual circumstances are screaming *stop*!
> Consolidate! I wanted to speak to Paul, but he's not well and
> I just have to listen to what God says.
>
> Ecclesiastes 11:4 says it all: "Whoever watches the wind will
> not plant; whoever looks at the clouds will not reap."
>
> We will not hold back because we have no money. We've
> never had any money and it has never stopped us. We will
> continue to act as if money was no object and God will deliver
> us from this place of famine and hardship. *No surrender*!!

This word has been a regular source of encouragement for us at
CAP. It speaks to me and says it never looks like it is the right
time to do anything. It always looks like it's all over. What we can
see will always put us off doing things. Praise God for His word
and the way so many have stood with me and sown when it
looked hopeless. It's part of the DNA God has given us and this
was about to set off a chain of events that was to be a defining
point in the history of CAP.

I can and do have moments of doubt and fear. I don't fight them
as much now. I know that when we come to an end of our own ability to keep going it is when God intervenes and rightly gets the glory.

Giving up or turning back was never an option, hundreds of
families relied on us for their future hope. In a nutshell we were
in a place of total reliance on God with no alternative other than
to hang on in there. Our wonderful clients needed us. We couldn't

simply stop and abandon them. However hard it was for us it was even harder for them.

October 31, 1999

In the midst of all that is going on it's still the families and the amazing changes we see that drive me forward. The work itself is absolutely wonderful. People are getting saved almost every week. We are growing in ability, confidence and drive to move forward despite our financial worries and difficulties. The word says it is impossible to please God without faith. Well in that case, He should be very pleased with us.

A defining moment in the history of CAP

Before we move on, I want to say that although we are very confident in where we are and where we are going, we are open to contrary opinions, counsel and other people's ideas and wisdom. Throughout the years, trustees, church leaders and friends have often challenged and questioned what we want to do. The trustees have said 'no' and the senior management team very much work on a consensus opinion. In particular, Paul Hubbard has often checked our strategies and asked difficult questions. I believe this strength of the senior management has been a great asset in terms of our advancement and confidence in the decisions we make. However, as you will see, when the very core faith of who we are and how we operate was challenged the faith and "nevertheless" spirit and unity of purpose and belief that rose up was a wonder to behold.

November 8, 1999

A very difficult time at present, a series of pressure points have left me in a terrible state. God is obviously moving through our work. Over the last two weeks we have seen a massive increase in people coming to know Jesus at our church. On Sunday at least two people gave their lives to Jesus and another four were at church. Deep down I know we are on the right track. Last month 45 families came through CAP. That's an amazing increase and we are starting to press forward. Only one centre is struggling in terms of clients and we know that God will sort that out, especially as such wonderful people are involved.

The difficult time I'm having is somehow more difficult because I see such success when I look at our results – the clients. On Friday one of our staff at a centre had the most horrendous conversation with me. It was a mixture of moaning and outright hostility towards the way we operated the ministry. This person said that we were in a terrible place not being able to pay wages on time and that we were completely wrong about how we lived financially.

I was rocked down to my boots. How could someone whom we had stood by for months, and encouraged all the way, suddenly turn on us and express such hostility towards us? She was one of the first to be paid and we had done everything to make sure she was looked after.

This eventually proved to be the first centre we actually closed. A very painful experience for all concerned and it was to be repeated six times over the next three years. Each one was very difficult in many different ways. Although they were difficult times, we now see that perhaps it was God's way of keeping the vision clear. For each one we took some responsibility and tried to learn from our mistakes. They have shown us more and more that the relationship with the partner church and its leadership is the key to our work succeeding.

We have learned from each closure, and in hindsight, have

now built up a broader picture of the whole range of skills and qualities needed to be a successful manager and how difficult it is to pioneer a successful centre. We have made mistakes and let some people down; we were sometimes too quick to open centres. We have learned this lesson and I can say we have moved on. At the end of the day if you are moving forward and developing what you do, not everybody will be able or want to stay with you, it's just a part of moving forward; painful yet necessary.

November 8, 1999 continued

I am starting to exhibit classic signs of stress. It is strange. Many times I have trained and helped people to spot stress and here I am exhibiting all the signs. I have lost my appetite and am easily angered. I just feel numb.

The pressure on Lizzie is also growing, She is wonderful and understanding and she does try to understand how I am so easily upset and have such mood swings. I was almost unable to go to work today. It's just too much to bear on my own and I went and opened up with Matt, Josie and Paul, that I was in a desperate place and they were totally with me and just held me up in prayer.

When will the pressure be released, what is God trying to hone in me that is still lacking and holding me back? I feel lost. My faith has wobbled over the last few days. I even thought that I could not face another member of staff not getting paid.

I have repented of my sin of lack of faith however the evidence against God intervening is growing. The thought of having to carry on and on with such a lack of finance leaves me wondering if I have got enough within me to sustain another few years.

Psalm 102 speaks of a man destitute. Verse 17 says: "He will respond to the prayer of the destitute; He will not despise their plea." Verse 13b says: "For it is time to show favour to her; the appointed time has come."

Oh, if this was the appointed time for God to reveal his abundance of provision to CAP.

I have learned over the years to be careful when opening up when I'm distressed. I have occasionally opened up with people who have either just quoted scriptures to me, or got depressed themselves and I've ended up ministering to them! As well as Paul and Lizzie, Matt and Josie Barlow have been a great source of encouragement. In four-and-a-half years they have never wavered or lost faith in what we are doing. They have that ability to stand with me and know what to say. I praise God for them and others for the way they have stood with me through all that you are reading about.

In the midst of my distress, when I was at my weakest, a huge test was to come upon us . . .

November 12, 1999

Another terrible day. I spoke to a trustee on the phone and I am absolutely devastated with the fact that it looks as if the whole heart of the charity is going to be changed. Everything I believe has been attacked. The trustee doesn't know, but by speaking out what he thinks it has tested me to the core.

He basically said it was wrong to move ahead when our finances are in such a bad way; that it can't be God's best and that we must now change how we operate. In real terms, we should change and become a ministry which responds when the money is in, rather than the other way round. This would include not opening any more centres, reducing staff and closing centres where there was insufficient finance within the church. One of his most cutting comments was that he felt the only thing that was distinctive about us, was that we never paid anything on time and were always struggling.

I am numb. The thought of giving up now fills me with pain. I have no real defence apart from FAITH and that's all I've got. In the world's eyes he is right. It looks foolishness to carry on hiring people and increasing centres when the factual evidence says there is no money.

I will just have to press on and hope God will bring it all through. At the end of the day CAP is His not mine but I will fight every inch of the way to keep the charity true to the foundations God has laid down within us.

November 19, 1999

What a week! I just came out fighting for what I believe is right. Something rose up in me that was from God. I somehow had an authority about what I said. I was so strengthened by God and His word. When I read the scriptures it was as if He had written them just for me – just for this moment.

1 Corinthians 3:10 speaks of the foundation God has laid through me and everyone should be careful how they build on these foundations.

Nehemiah 6:9, saying people will say the work will not be completed but I prayed to the Lord "Now strengthen my hands."

1 Chronicles 11:4, David was told he would not take the city, *nevertheless,* he captured the city.

Joshua 1:6–9, given to me early in CAP, reads that I should be bold and very courageous, and not depart from His word and will prosper.

I felt that I needed to state where I believed we were and how I felt we needed to pull together and remain in faith that God was with us. However, I understood that others may not agree and that I needed to know where everybody was.

During the week, I produced a letter and sent it out to all staff and trustees. All the trustees and staff have been asked to write to Paul Hubbard, (Chairman) with their thoughts. Did they agree with where we were going? Were they willing to stand with me? Did they think we should change?

The initial reaction was one of total support and encouragement. It appears that virtually everybody is with me in how we are doing and it was only this one trustee who had huge reservations.

I am so pleased with what God has placed within this ministry. We will succeed and press on. I pray that God will bring people to a heart connection.

Praise God for his strength. I somehow know that it's not all over and I know we will be pressed and tested over the coming weeks but nevertheless, with this kind of unity the work will be completed.

November 22, 1999

Over the weekend I received a letter from the trustee. Quite a difficult letter for me to read. He basically states that he disagrees with how we have developed the ministry and that he does not share my view that we must press on. It's always more difficult to deal with things when they are written down. You find yourself re-reading them.

I agree that if you look with your eyes it looks pretty grim. I say that if you look in faith it looks great. I could not reply to his arguments because logically speaking he was right.

We had a fantastic prayer meeting on Friday. Wonderful words of encouragement and of faith. Everywhere I turn there is encouragement that we are right to just have faith that God will see us through. Not for the first time *Word For Today* on Sunday was spot on. It said exactly what I've been on about. It even quoted Nehemiah.

Even the beginners Bible on Sunday morning TV had me amazed about how faith works against what the world would see. Jesus in a boat. The disciples thought it would sink and they woke Jesus up. Jesus said I sent us out in the boat. It won't sink because I'm in it! Again Lazarus was *dead* and in a tomb. It looked as hopeless as it can get. Jesus raised him to life to show His glory. It's the same with CAP. Jesus sent us out. He is in the boat so it will not be overwhelmed.

We agreed to press forward and believe that God would vindicate us. We were to ultimately lose one trustee. To re-read just how God intervened still takes my breath away, and this was, in some ways both the lowest and most crucial 'tipping point' of the ministry that I can recall.

The unity and strength of character that was forged in this dark period has laid a foundation of faith, togetherness and a 'nevertheless' spirit that God has used time and time again over the years to bring Him glory. The next entry is testimony to people doing extra special things to help us and I pray everyone who helped us, with perhaps no knowledge of our predicament, is encouraged by the result. As you will now see after we had made our stand God intervened in the most amazing way. *(Praise God for his faithfulness)*.

December 31, 1999

A month of continued pressure and God's intervention. No money came in for the first two weeks and we needed £35,000 to pay November and December's wages and clear our outstanding bills. Then in one week £30,000 came in. Firstly our application to Lloyds TSB came through for £10,000, then I rang Howard Bell, Chief Executive of Provident Financial Plc and asked him if he would let us have the £10,000 they were due to give us in March three months early. He was, as always, very understanding and after speaking with a couple of the other directors they agreed. Regular giving and one-off gifts began to come in so we were £10,000 short. Then on the Saturday – two weeks before Christmas – I got a Christmas card from a lady, who has been wonderful in supporting us over the years, and here was a cheque for £10,000! Yet again at the very last minute God provided miraculously.

The greatest encouragement over the last month is that we have begun to really push through in our Bradford centre with people getting saved and accepting Jesus as their personal Saviour. Three people got saved in the last month alone and began to have fellowship with us at church. This is what drives us on to press forward because people's lives are at stake. Each one of these people is very precious to God, whatever price we pay they are worth it. I see this as one way the Lord continues to reaffirm that we are in His will.

Wow! What a month and what a turnaround. We brought every-thing up to date and only occasionally over the next three years did we ever return to such a continual and lengthy time of need. The figures we needed have got bigger but we remain to this date together in our resolve to press on and I pray we never have to go through such a time as that again.

I believe that through these very difficult three months, God tested our resolve and established a core faith and values within who we are, what we do, why we do it and these core values will continue to bear much fruit.

Things settled down a bit and we concentrated on our new centres that were due to open. We continued to develop the support systems and in April, CAP was finally to leave Norland Gardens, the house where it all began four-and-a-half years previously. Praise God we actually covered the balance on the mortgage. We relocated CAP to Midland Road Bradford, which was basically an industrial unit. Some may recall my office, which was basically a broom cupboard with just breeze block on three walls and a small door. But to us it was great, twice as big as Norland Gardens had been.

The next five months saw the charity continue to grow from strength to strength; more centres, more staff and a steady increase in clients helped and more people getting saved.

It seems God really uses these crunch points. They are a bit like the pain of childbirth. They are really hard going at the time but they produce good results, bring our goals into sharp focus and help us to learn more of His power.

We now jump forward to 2002 because I want to show you how God came through in this way again for us.

It started with a simple spreadsheet I did with Janice Calvert who heads up our financial administration department. It was February and it showed – to our shock – that we needed just over £144,000, in addition to all our regular and known gifts, by our year end in May if we were to finish up to date.

We had never looked at our needs over three months before and maybe we should have left ourselves in blissful ignorance. It meant that if everything we knew was due to come in came in, and we spent what we thought we would, we would still need £144,000 extra. By April, things were getting, shall we say, a bit tight, though we had seen continual miracles of provision and we were down to needing £105,000. However, we were actually two-and-a-half months behind with wages and needed £80,000 right then!

I remember actually putting £30,000 on the spreadsheet in absolute belief that a trust I had applied to would give that amount to us.

April 2, 2002

It is eight weeks before our year end. The unthinkable has happened. I've got an awful email from someone I know very well. He's been such a generous supporter over several years.

In paraphrase he says: "We don't think it's right to give you any money. You are in a mess and need to change what you do."

It was just a few lines but it was quite harsh. He and his wife genuinely care for me and I know he has written this because he must have honestly believed it was for my good. I am shocked.

I have turned to God's word and asked him for grace to get me through.

He has given me Psalm 40. In particular verse 4a–b:

"Blessed is the man who makes the Lord his trust, who does not look to the proud."

Verse 11 summed up how I am feeling.

"Do not withhold your mercy from me, O Lord; may your love and your truth always protect me. For troubles without number surround me . . ."

Verse 13a: "Be pleased, O Lord, to save me;"

Verse 17: "Yet I am poor and needy; may the Lord think of me. You are my help and my deliverer; O my God, do not delay."

Psalm 41:1 says: "Blessed is he who has regard for the weak; the Lord delivers him in times of trouble."

As we moved into May, the trustees and the senior management team, Matt and Josie Barlow and myself spent an agonising time. Was God telling us to ask the staff to forego wages? This was such a difficult one. Yet, we just prayed and sought God. By May 15, with miracle after miracle of money coming in and a really successful mail out to our supporters we were down to just needing £48,000.

Former client and now National Prayer Co-ordinator Debbie Thompson, wrote down what she felt the Lord was saying. She had been led to Numbers 20:1–12 and Deuteronomy 32:51. It's the bit where the Israelites were in a desperate place and God said speak to the rock. Moses in verse 8 takes matters into his own hands and hits the rock. Water did gush out but God was not pleased because Moses had not trusted and done what God had commanded him to. The consequences of taking things into his own hands were very serious not only for him but the people he led. Later God says in Numbers 20:12–13 to Moses and Aaron. "Because you did not trust in me enough to honour me as holy in the sight of the Israelites, you will not bring this community into the land I give them. These were the waters of Meribah . . ."

She felt strongly that we should not ask staff to forego wages and just wait and trust in God. It was also noted: "Why do we have to get completely up to date for May 31, 2002 when we have virtually never been up to date!" Yes, thank you Josie for that one! However, our accounts are very important for many reasons and we believed it was a godly goal we had prayed and sought since February.

Well, we were overwhelmed with the amazing outpouring of generosity from our group of supporters. More than 500 people gave additional gifts. Almost every day we received cheques from a few pounds to a few thousand pounds. Each one came from a person who believed our vision.

On May 31, 2002 – our year end – we were just £24,000 short of our target. And by June 14, just 14 days after our year end, everything was paid up to date.

What an awesome God we have! I praise God for the men and women of God who surround me and have the strength to stand against such overwhelming circumstances that say we should cave in.

The results for the year end were astonishing. Almost every week someone was saved as a direct result of our work. We had helped 2,139 people in the year and had 25 centres working with local churches.

They had been testing times but these defining moments in CAP's history were over and we could now press forward into our future destiny.

CHAPTER NINE

THE WORK GOES ON

Back to January 2000

We opened three new centres in Blackburn, Alloa and Dunfermline. Things rumbled on over issues of funding and Trustees etc. but our relationship with one pastor in particular began to improve and the work just carried on. We continued with concentrating on getting people to know about Jesus. We continued with the fellowship evening at our house where we invite CAP clients for an informal meal and an introduction to our work and more and more people got saved.

Over the years we must have had over a hundred CAP clients through our house. It's been one of our greatest encouragements to hear first-hand how lives are changed. Throughout the country each centre does social events to allow clients to meet staff in a relaxed environment.

Here is just one testimony from Donna . . .

I had been a Christian since I was 13 but it meant very little to me. I didn't really understand what it was all about. But I knew God loved me and there was always a small part of me that knew Jesus.

Our story started for me back in 1998. I was 21 and pregnant with Teigan. I was living virtually alone and my partner was not supporting me other than a small amount for food. Things were difficult and I had been using catalogues to buy clothes for the new baby and me. Then suddenly it all just got out of hand. I just could not afford the weekly payments to the catalogues. This meant I had no spare money and the cycle of borrowing more and more to simply stand still just got out of control.

I felt lonely with no family nearby. I had no idea where the money was going to come from. Then one day a collector said that I could go to prison if I didn't pay what he wanted. I now realise this was ludicrous but on my own, seven months pregnant, I actually believed that I might be in prison when my baby was born.

I had met Gillian Clarkson through the Bierley Bethel Church in Bradford and she had taken me under her wing and told me that I should contact Christians Against Poverty. I was so scared I couldn't ring, so Gillian made the first contact.

Ruth Barber (Bradford Caseworker) started to help me. It was just like a huge weight was taken off my shoulders. Instead of paying £100 a week to four catalogues Ruth negotiated with every one of them and I paid just £10 a week. For the first time in years I could afford to buy food, clothing and everything I needed and pay my debts off slowly without people hassling me. I stopped borrowing because I had no reason to carry on, there was food on the table and I could live a reasonable life after I had paid into my CAP budget account.

Over the next two years I got myself completely sorted out, all my debts paid off and I was living within my means.

Then in 2000 I met my now husband Steven at a CAP celebration evening. Stephen was also a CAP client who had had similar difficulties and he had become a Christian through CAP. We hit it off straight away and before long we had fallen in love. We both understood just what the other had been through and it gave us a closeness we have had since the day we met. We both had complicated past relationships and children but somehow it all fitted together.

Stephen was basically forced into bankruptcy due to the Child Support Agency and spiralling debts. He tried for two years to avoid this drastic action but eventually he had no option. Even then CAP helped him with his fees and were with him through the whole harrowing experience.

Steve and Donna's CAP wedding

We married on the 23rd March 2001, and since then we have had a beautiful daughter, Millie Grace and we are managing our finances really well. We just managed to get a second-hand, seven-seater car to fit all our combined children in so we can all go out together.

We have had ongoing difficulties over the last 18 months. Stephen had job difficulties yet God and the church family have been so supportive. Stephen is due to finish his qualifications as an electrician in August 2003, and we are excited and want to get our own home over the coming year.

(Stop press: Stephen passed and got a full time job in September 2003.)

We find it hard to put into words just how much CAP has impacted our lives. Thank you seems so poor. Not only am I debt free, found a true and real faith and relationship with Jesus, I also found a wonderful husband as well and Millie Grace was the icing on the cake. The first CAP clients' baby!

I just want to say to people who pray and give to CAP, keep on giving and praying because it's such a worthy cause. There are so many people, just like Stephen and me, who desperately need what CAP has to offer. If people hadn't have given to help CAP back in 1998, Ruth and CAP would never have come into our lives. That's such a scary thought. Where would we have been? It doesn't bear thinking about.

Donna, Stephen and Millie.

February 2000

We realised that in the last eight weeks alone over ten people had become Christians through our work and we began to see that God was opening people's hearts to hear the good news. Things are really starting to get moving with the casework and I am beginning to see the fruit of all our hard work with the various departments.

Operations department, led by Matt Barlow, is really getting to grips with empowering centres to move forward with the vision. Budget accounts are growing as is an ever increasing number of clients responding to our work. Insolvency continued to move ahead and we are seeing more and more breakthroughs. Fund-raising, led by Josie Barlow, is starting to really get to grips with increasing the grace of giving. More and more regular givers were coming forward and we have begun to see our overall financial situation get better although our needs for January wages again did not materialise.

March 4, 2000

Another one of those crunch times. We need £20,000 just to cover February's wages and yet again our personal financial situations just get worse. It's somehow difficult to describe how we just press on for so long almost ignoring the reality of our plight only to be hit almost by surprise by how dire our plight looks. Even when I do get paid, my standing orders for all the basics like rent, utilities, life insurance, maintenance, tithe and other giving take the whole lot. We have just £3.44 left, we live from week to week on the rent money we get through the people who rent part of our old house and yesterday we learnt they are leaving in three weeks. The immediate situation is that I have literally nothing and we owe over £375. The contradictions and challenges in God's provision have never been starker.

Where is God in all this? The work is wonderful – more and more people are being saved and released from poverty. We expect to open five more centres over the next three months and yet financially it is as black as ever.

Why after nearly four years of struggle and strife driving on in

God's anointed work, releasing hundreds of people from poverty, pressing on with ever increasing faith, are we still as much in need as ever before? Why are our personal circumstances so dire when we have tithed and given away so much of whatever God has given us? Why are our debts rising whilst we are working to reduce others? Why are we saving hundreds from losing homes to being placed in such a position ourselves? You don't get many testimonies like this one on TV or in books.

(I obviously never thought this testimony would be in a book, which makes me laugh.)

Where is God? Why is it like it is? Will it carry on for the rest of our lives? Are we destined to always be in such financial needs as the ministry grows? Will our witness always be late wages, rising bills, massive daily needs? Only God knows, all I can do is say I have no option but to just carry on with what I know is right. I'm confused but I know that it will all become clear when we eventually meet face to face.

I left this in as I feel God already knows how we feel and it's not a news flash to him that we are 'a little' annoyed and confused. He is a real God who understands us when we talk openly about how we feel. Please do not be offended. God isn't.

Needless to say the money came in, in God's time.

CHAPTER TEN

CAP AUSTRALIA

October 1999

> During the last week God has shown me His sense of humour.
> Several months ago I met a guy called Warren Turner from
> Australia who was opening a mortgage and debt reduction
> company in the UK. We met and got on very well, in fact, he
> agreed to tithe the profits from his UK operation to the charity.
> He took some information about CAP and I almost forgot he'd
> said he would share my work with friends back in Australia.
> Now out of the blue I have an email from him saying he has
> shared my vision and our work with a church and a close Pastor
> friend. He now feels he wants to fly Lizzie, Abigail and myself to
> Australia for a four-week holiday next April and give me a
> chance to share the vision with some friends! It seems that they
> want to meet with me and see if they could duplicate our work
> in Australia! Who knows what God is doing?

Warren – fondly known at CAP as Wazza – and I had been introduced in February 1999 thanks to the most amazing set of God-
inspired events. Warren has a very specialised mortgage/
budgeting company in Australia which works with people to

reduce debt, increase assets and improve lifestyle and he had recently started the company in the UK.

He started the company in Bradford and had to pick some accountants. He picked the same as CAP. He then had to pick a specific accountant. He picked Trevor Milner a wonderful godly accountant who looked after CAP's accounts for the first six years.

He made an appointment to see Trevor and it just happened to be the next one after I had been to see Trevor and I had left a CAP newspaper for Trevor to read. Trevor for some unknown reason left the newspaper on his desk, (anybody who knows Trevor will know of his legendary tidiness and it must have been God for him to leave anything on his desk!) Warren sat down and picked up the paper and started to read it. He asked who we were, and Graham Newby who was with him and knew me through Ruth Graves, said he would bring Warren to see us. I am amazed at the lengths God will go to bring people together.

Warren visited us and was amazed at what we were doing, he even said he would tithe the profits from his UK business to CAP. Unlike many before and after him, he with Graham Newby and Richard Purnell, did actually honour this commitment and it has carried on ever since.

Then this fabulous offer came for an all-expenses paid trip for all of us to Australia for a four-week holiday and to share the work of CAP with a few brothers. Things like this just don't happen to me. Warren said he would make sure all our needs were met including spending money, car, a holiday apartment etc.

We were to meet Terry Cahill and Paul and Linda Scarfe, the Pastors of a church in Cardiff, a suburb of Newcastle NSW. Wazza thought these were the people who just might be able to take CAP Oz forward. Newcastle is a large industrial town two hours north of Sydney. It has had a declining steel industry and is similar to Bradford in both size and social demographics.

So in April 2000 off we went leaving much need at home, but after four years we needed the break. The first thing to say about Wazza, Terry Cahill, and Paul and Linda and their wonderful church called Contemporary Christian Centre (CCC) is that they delivered everything they said they would.

These people were different. They had a spirit of excellence in all they did. They did everything they said they would do, right down to having a car with a car seat and getting a high chair for Abigail.

Over the years so many people have said they would do things to help us and never have. Its such a shame when people over promise and under deliver, we should always be very careful not to say we will do this or that if we can't, or just forget that we promised. As Christians our witness should be one of faithfulness in all our dealings.

Our welcome was wonderful and the way they ministered to us left a real impression on both Lizzie and myself. I shared the vision for CAP and they just went for it. I found myself working closely with them and had to have all our training manuals emailed over. In two weeks we trained, envisioned and equipped them and CAP Australia was up and running.

I knew that it would need a people of passion, determination and drive to get this new branch of CAP going. Through prayer and time with the Lord, I decided to step back a bit when I got back to the UK to allow them to make it theirs and find their own identity. They did just that and over the next two years they worked very hard. Their finances were difficult but in the people close to the work, there was a real sense of ownership and sowing both financially and in time and effort.

After two years of them testing the procedures and actually

learning how CAP works, I returned in March 2002 on my own for a whistle-stop two-week visit. I worked with Terry and the team to help them set up systems so they could expand the work. While I was there they opened their first two CAP centres, which meant they had three operating when I left. They were such a blessing to me; their enthusiasm, commitment, hard work and their desire to see the lost saved took my breath away.

Terry, Paul and Linda have visited us here in the UK and seen how we work and together with Wazza they have very much been embraced as part of the whole CAP family. Wazza still visits the UK twice a year and continues to provide the link in terms of my relationship with him and the vision of CAP, which he holds very dear. He also played a major part in our drive to buy Jubilee Mill (see chapter 11).

We have had Kathy Ingram working with us here in the UK for three months from September to December 2002. She has been learning more about our systems and procedures and has taken the heart of what we do back with her to Oz.

It's very rare a group of people stretch my faith but this lot have a real desire for the lost. I know they will achieve their vision of a CAP centre in every Australian city and we will continue to do what we can to help, guide and support them. They are truly a wonderful group of men and women – of character and of God. We hope they will provide a bridge for CAP into New Zealand.

I find it amazing that God would make something so wonderful happen from one man's obedience and a small group of people able to grasp a vision and make it happen. I pray that Wazza, Terry, Paul, Linda and the whole CAP Australia team are encouraged by the way they have ministered and encouraged many within CAP in the UK. I am so proud of what they have achieved and so delighted to be able to support such wonderful people.

From left to right: Warren Turner (Wazza, Trustee), Paul Scarfe (Chairman), Terry Cahill (Director), Linda Scarfe (Trustee), Ian Stansfield (Trustee), Geoff Gregory (Trustee)

In March 2003, I returned to spend three weeks working with the team out there. While I was there they opened four new centres taking their total to seven. All the staff travelled to a four-day conference where I was able to impart, not just the actual debt counselling, but also, the heart behind what we do. They also decided to move to some larger premises as they were about to overrun the church.

Whichever side of the world CAP is on it is about the same thing, changing lives 'one life at a time'. Here is a testimony from just one of over 200 people CAP Australia has now helped:

After a friend told me about CAP and what they had done for her, I decided to make contact and see if they could help me.

It took quite a while for me to get up the courage to make an appointment to see Terry (the centre manager) and I was so nervous I considered leaving as soon as I'd got there. My biggest debt was to a loan shark and I was paying him a large amount of interest.

I had been long-term unemployed after bringing up my two daughters Amanda and Erin as a single parent with great difficulty. My youngest Erin had been sick all her life and now has kidney failure. We had many visits to doctors in Newcastle and Sydney and with limited finances I was always struggling to find the fares to get her to doctor's appointments.

The difference in my life since approaching CAP has been dramatic. The prayer and encouragement I have received has enabled to me to re-enter the workforce which is a major breakthrough. In my previous efforts to increase my income I had taken shift work in Sydney (two-and-a-half hours by train). On one of these trips I was assaulted and because of the fear of attack I was unable to continue commuting. The long periods of unemployment and then the assault had destroyed my self-confidence but I am now back in the workforce in a call-centre and am off all welfare assistance.

I am attending the church where the CAP centre is located and also a mid-week cell with the CAP clients and church members. My daughter Erin has become a Christian through her involvement in the cell and she is enjoying a renewed life.

This year, I went on my first holiday for ages when I attended a Christian Conference in Queensland. The joy of arranging the motel and travel details and then paying for them from my savings, through my CAP budget account, was almost as good as the holiday.

I now have confidence as I look to the future as I am debt free, employed and have a network of caring people around me.

Diane.

It could be from anybody here in the UK. There's that same heart, same desperation, same need, same solution and – most importantly – same wonderful outcome.

Paul and Linda Scarfe came for a week visit in May 2003 and were able to see first-hand how we operate here in the UK. They were an amazing encouragement to what we do and went away with pages and pages of notes on what they want to implement back in Oz.

I can't help thinking back to the word which told me to "enlarge my tent". When God gave me the following Scripture I had never imagined He meant 12,000 miles away. But it has become a reality:

> "Enlarge the place of your tent, stretch your tent curtains wide, do not hold back: lengthen your cords, strengthen your stakes. For you will spread out to the right and to the left; your descendants will dispossess nations and settle in their desolate cities."
>
> *(Isaiah 54:2–3)*

I have always known never to underestimate the words given to me and as you will see from the appendix at the back of the book I meticulously check them with the Lord and record who gave me the word, when and the circumstances. It's such a testimony to God's ability to uphold us through His scriptures and how Christians can be used to pass on direct encouragement and direction from the Lord.

I would encourage anyone to make notes in their Bibles of words given and specific teachings that speak directly to you. I read every word I am given, test it as I understand it may not be for the "just now" but may hold a promise way beyond anything I can ever dream or imagine.

CAP Australia is one of those things. It's way beyond anything I could ever have imagined in those early and very difficult days back in 1996–1999. Praise be to God.

I have asked Wazza to give a personal reflection on how he has seen the whole thing develop and here are his thoughts.

Wazza writes . . .

When I first met John and Lizzie they were in this four to five bedroom house that was so jam-packed with people and computers and graphs and stats on the walls! It seemed to be so well organised and the atmosphere was electric. Their commitment to the poor and needy – a phrase that has become near and dear to my heart since meeting John – was so deep. Most of all it was the spirit of generosity. No spirit of poverty there! I was totally mesmerised with the whole concept. As soon as I saw it I knew I wanted to sow into that ministry.

When I got home to Australia I did not know where to start. It was bigger than I could handle and I knew that the Lord wanted the right people to head up CAP Australia, if there was to be one. I wish I could say that I prayed it through and thought about it down to the last detail. In truth, the Lord had his hand on it from the very start. I was invited to speak to a Christian business group about what I had seen and what my thoughts were. Among other people at that meeting were Terry Cahill and Paul Scarfe – two tremendous men of God with a passion for the poor and needy.

I knew that if Aussies could just listen to John and get a glimpse of what the vision was, they would be blessed and a fire would start in their hearts. I also felt that John and Lizzie had been such a blessing to so many people and it was right to bless them. John and Lizzie came for just a few weeks and the vision was caught and people's lives changed and people became totally committed to seeing the vision for CAP Australia become a reality.

In the first two years I personally was a little frustrated in the growth. We grew very slowly but by the end of the second year I understood why. It was so intense and there was so much to take in and so many systems to learn and skills to teach if we were to keep to the high standard in the UK. We wouldn't have been ready to handle any more. Our first budget was $50,000, the next was $350,000 and we all nearly had a coronary. But God is in control of the finances.

Now CAP Australia is getting integrated with the UK system and people are getting better at what they do. We are no longer getting a rap on the knuckles from John. That man has a lot of patience! We are seeing people's lives getting back together, being freed from debt. The future from CAP Oz is bright and exciting. Our vision is to take this nation one life at a time.

Bless you heaps

Wazza.

As we returned from Australia our fourth year came to a close. By May 2000, we had seen continued growth within the charity. We had seen the centre network grow to 12 and our relationships with the churches were getting much better. We were beginning to realise what were the important ingredients that made CAP centres work. We needed a church leader willing and able to embrace the vision and encourage his church to get involved, an individual who would really pioneer the work and drive the centre forward and prayer teams together with 'life changers' to make the whole thing work. Our income had increased from £157,460 to £310,053. We had helped just over 1,000 people in the year and we were in good heart.

CHAPTER ELEVEN

JUBILEE MILL

In September 2000, Operations Director Matt Barlow and I, took Wazza and Paul Hubbard away for three days to a magnificent Chateau-come-castle owned by the family of one of our greatest and longest supporters Jacqueline. We flew Easy Jet to Geneva, rented a car and settled in for what we had thought would be a time of prayer and reflection.

God had other ideas and we ended up sailing a beautiful, old, wooden sailboat up and down the lake at the bottom of the garden and just had a fantastic time together. There were barbecues on the lakeside, great meals out and trips around the most wonderful Swiss scenery. The place was called La Lance and it was a bit like the house in The Sound of Music with a garden sweeping down to a lakeside with a jetty and a boathouse.

One night we were having a meal when I got onto the fact that I was finding it very difficult to raise £250,000 to buy a building for the ever-increasing Bradford based CAP operation. We were in an industrial unit and my desk was in a basic breeze-block broom cupboard. We wanted out! Wazza said: "Why don't you use your business skills and put together some business proposal for investors?" He then shared his wisdom on how people could invest and be secure in their investment and that paying a return was not wrong as long as it furthered the charity work and the building purchased was the right one with potential to rise in value over time.

This really stuck with me and with hindsight I think that this was perhaps one of the main reasons we went away. At home or at work you never seem to get the time to just relax and allow God to direct your conversation through being with friends. Upon my return, I began to think about how and when I could step out in faith and try to find investors and a suitable property.

One man sprang to mind. His name was Bernard and he had a family trust that had supported us with a very large and much-needed grant over the previous year. I knew he was a very good and sharp businessman and that he would probably be open to such an unusual proposal.

I just happened to be due to stay with him a couple of weeks later and had prepared this amazing presentation about how he might invest some of the money in his trust, get a great return and help us out. There I was, sitting at his breakfast table, and I remembered how Nehemiah had asked God to help him when he was about to ask the King for favour. In chapter 2, verse 4, the King asks him: "What do you want?" Nehemiah just prayed to the God of heaven and spoke out what he wanted.

I just thought 'God will give me the words' and Bernard asked me what I wanted to ask him. I said: "Would your Trust invest £150,000 and help me buy a mill to redevelop as a home for CAP?" and before I even had chance to get my presentation out, he said "Yes!"

I will be eternally grateful for the vote of confidence Bernard showed me there and then and for his decisive reaction. It was within his power to help and he did not withhold that help. Armed with this I began looking for a suitable property and went to see a few.

After viewing one small mill, I saw a billboard out of the corner of my eye on a building and I rang up while we were going back to the office. The young lad at the agents said it was only 8,000 sq. feet but asked what I wanted. I said I wanted a large mill that I could develop. He suggested another agent he knew who was selling an old mill through trustees in bankruptcy. I rang up and it was the old Bradford Box Makers Mill just within the ring road. It was on the market for £250,000 and was 38,000 sq. feet, over four floors.

I remember first turning the corner and thinking how beautiful it looked. It was actually a shell of a building that had been abandoned, stripped of all useful things and left to deteriorate. As soon as I walked in I knew this was it. I could see it. God gave me the vision and believe me, it had to be from God. I remember showing other members of the CAP team around and they have since confided in me that they thought I had completely lost my marbles. There was so much water on the ground floor you had to wear wellies and take an umbrella!

I knew this mill was bigger than the money Bernard said he would lend us, however undaunted, I rang the only other person I knew who might be able to help, Jacqueline, who had lent us her Swiss home a few weeks before. Although I knew her family trust was relatively small, I asked her the same question and would you believe it, only the week before I rang, there had been a pleasant surprise – the trust had recently received £50,000 of shares to invest.

Everything was still up in the air but I felt I now needed to press forward and make an offer. I got the figure to offer to buy it for just £185,000. This meant if we borrowed £235,000, in total, we would be left with £50,000 to start the huge task of beginning the redevelopment.

The agent was flabbergasted by how small the offer was. It worked out at just £5 per square foot to buy – less than many would pay to rent it! A day later he rang back and said the trustee in bankruptcy was very unhappy at my offer, however they would accept it. I rang Bernard up and he agreed to increase the loan to £185,000 and when I added the other £50,000 we had enough to buy it and do the immediate repairs and refurbishment to get seven offices for us to move into.

The next few weeks are very much a blur. We had to get contractors agreed, create loan agreements with undertakings to give the investors a share of the equity we had agreed to return to them. We had to get contractors to quote for the roof, the re-pointing and sandblasting of the walls. Margaret Upstone, who is my PA and great friend, worked with me and she did the most amazing job. I will never forget standing with Margaret knee-deep in water, with gloves and wellies on, ice on the inside of the building, talking to a roofer about getting the roof fixed.

We bought the mill in January 2001. The next two months God really moved and amazingly we were able to get seven offices ready so we could all move in March. One Saturday we had nearly 100 people cleaning out the mill. In total we took out over 100 cubic metres, 10 skip loads, of rubbish accumulated over the past 50 years.

The mill was renamed "Jubilee Mill" after the year of Jubilee in Deuteronomy where every seven years debts were cancelled. Over the last two-and-a-half years we have seen miracle after miracle. Our plan was to redevelop it in relatively small stages and rent bits out to generate income for future redevelopment and for the charity. We raised another £150,000 from other supporters and with money raised from trusts, we have now completed one half of the mill redevelopment. Four separate sections have been finished and all the units and offices are let out. We have also completed the top floor redevelopment, which has provided the extra space we have needed as we have continued to grow.

Our rental income is now £60,000 a year. After interest and ongoing maintenance this is providing £3,000 per month in regular income to the charity. Jubilee Mill was valued at £575,000 in May 2003, which has given us over £150,000 worth of equity. All this in just over two years! We still have over half of the mill to redevelop over the coming four years. We are always looking for people to lend us money to help this project and are due to launch a "Jubilee Mill Redevelopment Scheme" in Autumn 2003, whereby many other supporters will be able to help this project be completed by lending relatively small amounts to pay for ongoing redevelopment. For further information contact CAP.

Jubilee Mill, Bradford, Operations Centre

Our goal, by May 2006, is for rental income to reach £110,000 per year and for the mill to be worth over £1,250,000 putting over £400,000 of assets on our balance sheet. Not bad for a few days messing about in Switzerland and a nice meal with great friends!

I would like to thank every investor who made it possible, from the main investors to the people who volunteered to clean out the mill. I also want to thank Margaret Upstone, my PA for the last two-and-a-half years. She has been such a support with this whole project. There were so many things she knew nothing about but just "had a go at". She is a tremendous example of a woman of God, who uses what she has for the glory of God.

Jubilee Mill stands out as a testimony of what can be achieved when you have a vision from God, when people are willing to step out in faith and do what they can to help and when you all work hard over a long period of time to a specific strategic plan.

One of our greatest gifts in the whole Jubilee Mill story has been Clive Boldy. He has worked on and overseen each stage of redevelopment and is responsible for the ongoing maintenance. Clive was a CAP client who was released from terrible poverty, found Jesus, led his whole family to the Lord and now works full time for CAP. He is such a humble and hard-working man, whose only desire is to serve God any way he can. He has served us all and CAP very well in the process.

I want Clive to describe his story in his own words and how Jesus, through CAP, has completely transformed his life.

Clive writes . . .

It all started back in 1996, when I took a small loan out for second-hand car. Before that I had hardly ever used credit. I had never had a car before and the bills just started to come in and very slowly things began to get tighter with our finances. We began to borrow small amounts to repair the car, cover insurance and we also missed one mortgage payment.

Then I borrowed to keep up to date. Before I knew it we were in a spiral of having to borrow to repay ever increasing loans. Suddenly we were very poor.

I worked as an engineer and all my wages were spoken for before I got them. The hot-water boiler packed up and there was just no way I could afford to get it fixed. We went without hot water for two years, with four children aged 14, 13, 11 and 10. It was very hard especially as my pride would not let me tell anyone or ask for help. We had bought a house back in 1991, in an area that was not that bad, but over the years it began to go down. There were drug people outside and the kids and Cath could never go out alone and we became prisoners in our own home. Even if we could have gone out we never had enough money. We bought the house for £33,000 back in 1991 at the height of the housing boom, but now not only were we falling further and further behind with the mortgage but the house was only worth about £15,000 and we still owed over £33,000 and it was going up each month.

My health began to suffer as we were in such a dark place. My only relief was a weekly night out playing darts with my mates. Even then I had to borrow a few pounds for a drink.

After four years of this the crunch came in early 2000. I had a breakdown at work. I was found aimlessly walking around the lathe in a complete daze. People at work were good to me. They drove me home and I just collapsed. Cath phoned the doctor who said I had had a nervous breakdown and he sedated me and I slept for 24 hours.

I knew I had to do something so I went to a company I had seen advertised on the telly. They said they could help; however over the next six months things just got worse. They took our money but my debts just got bigger as they charged and didn't stop interest being added. I also had to still try and pay my mortgage. I was in a desperate situation. What could we do?

Then my sister gave me the most important piece of paper of my life – an information leaflet for Christians Against Poverty offering free debt counselling. Cath phoned and a week later Tim Griffiths (Bradford Caseworker) came round. After listening to our story and writing down all our information, the first thing he said was that he wanted to pray, which I thought was a bit strange. He then worked through all our debts. He took every piece of paper, bills, letters etc. and told me to leave it with him and if anyone was to ring or more letters came to just send them to him. It's impossible to describe just what a relief that was. He said: "Don't worry, we can sort this out if you will work with us." Four years of sheer hell were over. We were not alone and we had a hope.

Over the next three months Tim contacted all our creditors and negotiated reduced payments and the results were spectacular. No more letters, no more collectors at our door and no more threatening phone calls. Tim set up a CAP budget account, where all our priority payments such as gas, electric, mortgage, council tax and all the agreed new loan repayments were to be made for us. All we had to do was pay into our budget account the agreed amount each week and we had enough money left to buy food and clothing for our family. What a difference! We even began to save a little and give a few pounds a month to CAP to help someone else like us.

I was then invited to an evening at John and Lizzie Kirkby's house where I met other people who were in the same boat. I also realised that these Christians were nice people and I started thinking about what life was really all about.

Tim then invited me to a Christian basics course run by Christian Life Church, Shipley (the Bradford partner church and where CAP started in 1996) *and after three weeks I gave my life to Jesus. Nothing magic happened. It just felt good. It felt like there was something for me to go on for.*

I told my work mates I had become a Christian and they ridiculed me and made a massive cardboard cross. I was so elated I just took it off them and put it above my machine. I felt like I was walking on air and nothing could take away the joy I felt inside.

Over the last two years my life has been utterly transformed. With CAP's help we negotiated to leave our home and get re-housed. The building society repossessed our house and sold it for a huge loss leaving me still owing them £24,000. CAP just got stuck in to the building society and eventually they agreed to accept just £1,500 as "full and final settlement" of my total debt of £24,000! What a miracle and only through CAP could that have happened.

Cath, my wife, and my children are all now Christians and we are together as a family at Christian Life Church. We also had our one and only family holiday in 2002, when we went away for a week to Bridlington and we took money we had saved up through our budget account. We had such a great time together as a family. We could afford some treats and the children were really blessed.

In June 2001, I gave my job up to help CAP in Bradford by driving a van to deliver household goods to poor people in the city. I had to take an £8,000 a year wage cut but I still had more money than I had ever had. Within just two weeks of joining CAP an opportunity came for me to head up the redevelopment of Jubilee Mill and I grabbed it with both hands.

Since then my life has continued to be a series of miracles. I have found the right place that God wants me to be. My future is bright and my only goal is to serve my brothers and sisters in this wonderful ministry of CAP. There is no way I could ever repay what they did for my family and me but I will keep trying.

I also want to say a massive thank you to everyone who has ever supported CAP. Without your support CAP would not have been able to help me and I can't even begin to imagine where we would have been now.

Once again thank you CAP and God for my new life.

Clive and Cath Boldy

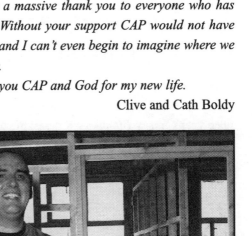

Clive working on top floor of Jubilee Mill, our new
Central Operations offices

CHAPTER TWELVE

INTO THE FUTURE

Each year *Charity Finance* – a magazine for the charity sector – stages a competition to find the best managed charities in the UK. In 2003, as we had two years previously, we submitted a written account of our management strategy and achievements. Then there was a trip to London to show to a distinguished panel of experts why we thought CAP should win the title for excellence in management. I was very pleased with the presentation and felt I did justice to CAP. We were informed we'd been short listed.

The night of the awards ceremony came and Paul Hubbard and I arrived at the Intercontinental Hotel in London. I really wanted to honour Paul, because he was the man who had led me to Jesus and had been so close to CAP over the preceding seven years. Various celebrities mingled with the crowd of 500 from the charity sector for the gala dinner. No one knew who had won so it was a tense night as we waited for our category, which was the last of the evening. The standard was so high that even to be short listed was tremendous. I knew the effort that we had put in over the last seven years and I so wanted it to be recognised for the staff and for anyone who had ever supported us. Also, to elevate our profile as a Christian charity, operating with excellence for His glory!

To keep the evening brief, each winner was allowed just four words with which to make their acceptance speech. When the host called out "Christians Against Poverty" I was so emotional. We were right at the back of this enormous hall and it took me ages to get to the stage. The whole of the previous years came back to me, the hardship, the difficulties and all we had been through. There was all this clapping and I was just thinking 'God we have come a long way together'. I realised that I was still as on fire for what the Lord had called me to those seven years ago and that the compassion He first gave me was burning even brighter than before.

My four words? "Thank You! Praise God!"

We had been previously beaten two years before in 2001, when we were short listed but lost. Winning the 'Charity of the Year Award for Excellence in Management' in the category 'Research, Advice and Support' was an amazing achievement and a testimony to the sheer hard work and commitment of the staff to give the poor the very best.

We remain totally focused and committed to giving the very best debt counselling to the needy free of charge. We so much want to continue sharing the good news of Jesus with people who are hurting. We have always approached our work with a great deal of care, attention to detail and always kept the vision and our certain knowledge that God wants us to expand and grow.

Behind the scenes there is an awesome group of dedicated people doing everything they can to see this thing succeed. CAP is a lot more sophisticated than it used to be and it will continue to need this attention to detail and drive for excellence if we are to achieve our vision.

Throughout the whole of the last seven years we have constantly re-examined how we work in every area of our operation in a bid to improve.

Each time we train 'raw recruits' to be centre managers, they seem to reach a high standard more quickly. It's true to say we have a culture of 'how can we do it better?', which has, continually pushed the charity into new dimensions.

Over just the last 18 months we have seen new centralised systems of negotiating with the finance industry on our clients behalf and a brand new computer account management system HOPE (Helping Oppressed People Everyday). Both these have revolutionised how we serve our clients.

As time goes on, we are gaining an ever-increasing reputation for professionalism and integrity within the finance industry.

Seven years have gone by since God and I started CAP and what takes my breath away is the speed with which God has grown this ministry.

As I sit in my top floor office in Jubilee Mill, with my view over Bradford, I am humbled by the statistics. We now have more than 60 people working for the charity and 30 centres based in local churches from Dunfermline, Scotland, in the North, to Aldershot in the south. We have seven centres open in Australia and signs that God may have plans for possible openings in other countries. We have received funding from more than 2,000 individuals – many I don't even know. Our turnover has gone from £10,000 in 1996–1997, to over £860,000 in this last year. In total, we have seen just over £2.7 million come in and we started with £10!

The CAP staff summer 2002 conference

Over 6,000 individuals have asked us for help, thousands of these have been released out of the misery of poverty and debt and over 250 of them have found the Lord through our work. The awesome sense of God in what we have done is almost overwhelming.

It is staggering what God can do with ordinary men and women who put their trust in Him.

Recently, I was drawn back to this word the Lord gave me some time ago, in Deuteronomy 11:8–16 and 22–25. It speaks of moving into a new land.

> "It is a land the Lord your God cares for; the eyes of the Lord your God are continually on it from the begining of the year to its end". (v12)
> ". . . the Lord will drive out all these nations before you, and you will dispossess nations larger and stronger than you. Every place where you set your foot will be yours . . . No man will be able to

stand against you. The Lord your God, as He promised you, will put terror and fear of you on the whole land wherever you go". (vv23, 25)

I believe we are simply at the beginning of an even more amazing story that will follow this one. We will see our vision of 50 centres within the next five years and over 250 by the year 2020, one in every major town and city in the UK.

This vision and our progress is simply too big for us to have made it up ourselves, yet we just believe with the Lord's help it will happen. There is so much need in this country – and indeed around the world.

Millions of people – and you might be one of them – are only a period of sickness, another loan, another credit card, another hire purchase away from a spiral of debt, poverty and misery.

However, we understand that we will have to continue to get even better at what we do, to remain focused on the wonderful people we have the privilege of serving. We will need hundreds, and then thousands, of ordinary people to decide to support us in our work.

Thank you for joining us on this journey. My prayer is that you will be inspired and moved by stories of people like Denise and Dennis, Clive, Debbie, Donna and Steve, and thousands more untold stories.

We need your prayerful and financial support to make a difference. Join with us today in this awesome God-inspired vision – complete the "Life Changer" form at the back of this book.

Our faith remains a "nevertheless" type of faith that God will continue to supply all we need. This includes all the future staff, partner churches and supporters and the continued financial miracle we need each day, week and year to advance our vision.

The driving force behind all we do, remains the same today as it was back in 1996 . . . God's heart of love and compassion poured out for the poor and needy – to see His salvation break out and lives transformed.

I hope you have been inspired and encouraged to do what you can to advance the Kingdom of God. I would like to leave you with the word that I believe the Lord has for all of us and remains so relevant for those working at CAP and our clients.

To Him be all the glory, honour and praise.

"Now to Him who is able to do immeasurably more than all we ask or imagine, according to His power that is at work within us, to Him be glory in the church and in Christ Jesus throughout all generations, for ever and ever! Amen."   *(Ephesians 3:20–21)*

PROPHETIC WORDS GIVEN AND RECEIVED DURING THE FIRST SEVEN YEARS OF CAP

The following are words I have received which have been of great direction and encouragement. I thank God for the many who brought me words and for His openness to me whenever I called upon Him for strength, guidance, encouragement and faith to simply carry on.

3rd January 1996
Jeremiah 29:11–13

> **Personal reflection** Just three months before I was to give up my job, the Lord clearly told me he had plans for me that would prosper me and not harm me. Praise God for his promise right at the start before I had any idea of what was to follow.

9th March 1996
Luke 4:18–19

> **Personal reflection** The spirit of the Sovereign Lord is upon me. I felt the Lord saying he would anoint me to work with the poor releasing them and proclaiming the Gospel before the vision of CAP was birthed. This was the day I started the process of giving up my job, unsure about exactly what I was to do for God.

March 1996

Ezekiel 18:8–9

> **Martin Parker** Speaks of CAP weeks before I got the real direction for the ministry.

March 1996

Luke 9:62

> **Personal reflection** It's a word which says that once I start the process and resign there is no looking back.

In June 1996 I spent four weeks in the word, praying about what it says with regard to the poor and needy. Here are the main Scriptures.

June 1996

1 Chronicles 29:1–14

> **The launch month** Speaks of outrageous provision for the building of God's temple. God will provide through others generosity when they understand the heart of what we do.

June 1996

Leviticus 25:35–38

> **The launch month** Initial investigation into CAP speaks of God's rules in finance, not charging interest etc. We will try to get interest stopped on all debts people owe.

June 1996

Deuteronomy 15:4–11

> **The launch month** Original word and study re: CAP speaks of God's desire that we give and that there will always be poor in the Land – no shortage of people needing help with debt and poverty.

June 1996

Deuteronomy 24:10–13

> **The launch month** Original word study re: CAP. Speaks of Gods laws re: finance.

June 1996

2 Kings 4:1–7

The launch month William Spencer. Word given to William about CAP saying the oil would never run out as long as we kept bringing empty jars. Little did we know that seven years later we would still have many jars empty just waiting for the Lord to fill them!!

June 1996

Proverbs 22:9

The launch month Says a generous man will himself be blessed as he shares his food with the poor.

June 1996

Proverbs 22:22–23

The launch month Says how we should not exploit the poor and how God will uphold them and plunder those who plunder them. Of Gods protection of the poor.

June 1996

Proverbs 28:27

The launch month He who gives to the poor will lack nothing. (Praise God).

June 1996

Proverbs 29:7

The launch month Says the righteous care about justice for the poor.

June 1996

Proverbs 31:8–9

The launch month This is the Proverb on which CAP is founded. "Speak up for those who cannot speak for themselves, for the rights of all who are destitute. Speak up and judge fairly; defend the rights of the poor and needy." We are still doing this today seven years later.

June 1996

Isaiah 10:1–4

The launch month Speaks against oppression.

June 1996

Isaiah 25:4

> **The launch month** Start of CAP says we will be a refuge for the poor, a place of shade. Speaks of how difficult it is when people are oppressed and in need.

June 1996

Isaiah 33:15–16

> **The launch month** Start of CAP says if we are strong and make the right decisions we will be supplied with all we need.

June 1996

Isaiah 61:1– 4

> **The launch month** This is the word that CAP was and is founded upon in terms of why we do what we actually do, and who provides the spirit needed to do it all. Also speaks of the hope for the people we help.

June 1996

Ezekiel 34:4–14

> **The launch month** Just as CAP was starting, says how we will bring back the strays and heal the weak and the sick.

June 1996

Matthew 6:25–34

> **The launch month** This speaks of not worrying, and that I just need to seek God first and every thing else will follow. This was and is a basic belief that underpins and sustains us over the years, whenever we are under pressure and in great need we try and remember not to worry, but seek him.

June 1996

Luke 21:2–4

> **The launch month** The widow's two small coins. Spoke to me of the value of people's support to CAP not in terms of the amount they give but the heart behind each gift. Also that every penny was precious.

June 1996

Philippians 3:12–15

> **The launch month** About forgetting what is behind and straining forward to what is ahead. This has been a source of great encouragement to me over the years. Great exaltation for us all to press forward into all God has for us.

June 1996

1 John 3:16–19

> **The launch month** At the start of CAP it speaks of us giving material possessions to others in need and that we should love with our actions not our words. This was part of establishing CAP as a practical outworking of the love Jesus has placed within us.

June 1996

Exodus 22:25–29

> **The launch month** About Finance system, that God will hear people's cries when they are in distress.

June 1996

Hebrews 11:1

> **The launch month** The great faith statement. "Now faith is being certain of what we hope for and certain of what we do not see." This has been my word from God for the whole of my time with him. Faith is a gift but it must be used to increase.

2nd July 1996

Ecclesiastes 11:1– 6

> **Personal reflection** Right at the start of CAP saying we should always be prepared to ask people to help us "cast our bread upon the water" v4 speaks of planting when it looks the wrong time. This was vital in establishing the faith element of CAP and encouraging us to step out every time even though it always looks the wrong time. Praise God.

2nd July 1996

Isaiah 55:10–11

> **Personal reflection** Says His word will not return without accom-

plishing what it was sent for. Felt this was a confirmation to make sure his word was included on all our documentation, literature etc.

July 1996

Isaiah 58:9–12

> **William Spencer** Just at the start of CAP. They are wonderful verses speaking about what CAP will do in removing poverty and destitution

6th September 1996

1 Chronicles 28:20

> **Personal reflection** First few days of CAP. "Be strong and courageous" and "Do the work" speaks of God being with me and all I have to do is "the work". Amazing word so early on when CAP was literally a few days old.

19th September 1996

Romans 5:1– 5

> **Personal reflection** Says we should rejoice in our sufferings and that hope does not disappoint.

19th September 1996

James 1:2–8

> **Personal reflection** Again saying we should consider pure joy when we face many trials. Not quite reached pure joy!!

23rd September 1996

Jeremiah 17:5–8

> **Personal reflection** On the night I got a letter saying I was wrong and should stop doing what I was doing. Felt the Lord say not to fear man but to fear Him. This laid down a foundation of not being intimidated by man and not fearing what men thought. Praise God, I was to need this word many times from that day on.

11th October 1996

Isaiah 45:3

> **Charles Price** Treasures in Darkness. CAP just started and already very tough.

17th November 1996

Psalm 28:8

> **Martin Parker** Says the Lord is our strength, this was during the first few months of CAP how right Martin was!!

17th November 1996

Proverbs 28:8

> **Martin Parker** Speaks of the wealth of money lenders being given to another who will help the poor.

November 1996

2 Chronicles 31:2–20

> **Personal reflection** Speaks about people bringing in the tithe and that there is no lack, in fact there is abundance. This is how it should be for CAP if we struggle financially we will never blame God He has blessed people enough to give for all our needs.

21st December 1996

Deuteronomy 8:17–18

> At the beginning of CAP. Very hard time. A promise that God had given me the ability to create wealth. (At the time I had nothing, £26,000 in debt, three months behind with my mortgage and no money for CAP). I had this word again in October 1998.

31st December 1996

Proverbs 31:8–9

> **Personal reflection** The original Proverb upon which CAP is founded. A timely reminder as I began to realise just what difficulties we were to face.

31st December 1996

Isaiah 25:4

> **Personal reflection** Reminded me of the pressure the poor and needy feel and that I was a refuge for them.

31st December 1996

Luke 4:18–19

> **Personal reflection** The spirit of the sovereign Lord is upon me. I felt

the Lord reminding me that He had anointed me for the work I was undertaking.

31st December 1996

Revelation 2:26

> **Personal reflection** Speaks of authority having been given to the ones who do his will.

9th January 1997

Jeremiah 22:16

> **Lawrence Greavsley** It says that the Lord will support those who defend the cause of the poor and needy.

22nd January 1997

Joshua 1:5–9

> **Angela Spencer** 8.09 am. Very low point. CAP only six months old. No money, totally rejected. This phone call was a wonderful word spoken right into my spirit by the Lord.

23rd January 1997

Matthew 7:24–25

> **Personal reflection** About to lose our house, God said build your house upon the rock, you will be secure.

28th January 1997

Isaiah 40:28–31

> **Avril Gray** Huge needs, no money, look like losing our home. Just as we put our house up for sale and all looked very bleak. It says we will soar on eagles wings and walk and not be faint. (Great word at a very difficult time).

1st February 1997

Psalm 16:1–10

> **Mona Bray** Difficult times, speaks of "the joy of the Lord is our strength".

1st February 1997

3 John 1:2

> **Mona Bray** That I would enjoy good health as my soul will prosper.

3rd February 1997

Psalm 23:1–6

> **Sue Dutton** Sue had a vision of God as our great shepherd.

18th February 1997

Zechariah 9:12

> **Derek Brown** Hold on and you will get a double portion.

18th February 1997

Ecclestiastes 4:9–12

> **Derek Brown** Right at the time we were starting to get going. I was on my own and felt the Lord say, get some people around, you will need them.

18th April 1997

Joshua 24:15–17

> **Personal reflection** As for my household, we will serve the Lord. A word of affirmation about our home.

29th April 1997

Psalm 91:2–14

> **Personal reflection** "He is my refuge and my fortress, my God in whom I trust," etc. Amazing Psalm of God's protection, love and total embrace.

2nd May 1997

Mark 14:8

> ***Word for Today*** Talks about a woman doing what she could do. I felt I was doing what I could do, God would do the rest.

2nd May 1997

1 Corinthians 1:27

> ***Word for Today*** For God chose the foolish things of this world to shame the wise . . .

2nd May 1997

Proverbs 22:22

Personal reflection Speaks of God upholding the case of the poor.

2nd May 1997

Proverbs 17:5

Personal reflection Says he who mocks the poor shows contempt for his maker.

2nd May 1997

Psalm 91:15–17

Word for Today "He will call upon me and I will answer him; I will be with him in trouble, I will deliver him and honour him . . ."

2nd May 1997

Genesis 39:20

Word for Today While Joseph was in prison the Lord was with him. (Praise God)

2nd May 1997

Proverbs 16:19

Personal reflection Speaks of the honour of being with the oppressed.

3rd May 1997

Philippians 4:10–13

Paul Hubbard This is about being content in plenty and in lack. This helped me deal with the hardships we faced in those early years as I tried to be content. Also confirmed that not having money was not a sign of God's disapproval. God did not disapprove of the apostle Paul and he was hungry and in lack.

May 1997

Joshua 1:5–9

Whilst at Pilgrim Hall leaders' conference, CAP less than one year old, all looks lost, losing house, no support!! "Be bold and courageous . . . Be strong and very courageous . . ."

May 1997

Judges 9:8–15

> **Ken Summerall** Speaks of God looking for leaders. Only me in CAP but felt the Lord saying he had anointed me as a leader!!

May 1997

Psalm 65:1–5

> **Derek Brown** Says we should be prepared to praise God before he turns up!

May 1997

Jeremiah 30:18–20

> **Bryn Jones** Speaks of God bringing honour to those who serve him and that He will add to their numbers.

6th June 1997

Jeremiah 30:18–20

> **Personal reflection** Speaks of God's sense of honour that will be bestowed on those who serve him.

7th June 1997

Psalm 37:25–34

> **Personal reflection** Says the righteous nor their children have ever had to beg for bread. We had very little money for food at this time, getting very tough.

16th September 1997

Jeremiah 15:19–21

> **Derek Brown** Speaks of the fact that we will be overcomers, although we can expect to be attacked and that He will rescue us from the enemy.

October 1997

Proverbs 15:22

> **Personal reflection** Says we need counsel to prevent things failing. (Something I have sought throughout the last seven years. I have just been careful in who's counsel I seek).

21st January 1998

Isaiah 45:3

> **Lorna** Difficult dark time. "I will give you treasures of darkness, riches stored in secret places."

March 1998

Exodus 3:4–5

> **Personal reflection** Speaks about not being afraid of your pain, and that you should share it as others need to know about it.

1st June 1998

Joshua 3:15–17

> **Personal reflection** Speaks of God's miraculous provision if we step out like priests crossing Jordan. A few people led a whole nation to get into the promised land!

September 1998

Deuteronomy 6:1–5

> **In America** A promise to possess land if we keep God's commandments. To love the Lord God with all your heart and soul and strength.

September 1998

Isaiah 54:2–4

> **Personal reflection** I received this word as we were on the verge of opening our very first centre. It was to become one of the most important words the Lord ever gave us. Stated that we would not be disgraced or humiliated. I only fully understood this many years later.

September 1998

2 Kings 2:19–22

> **Derek Brown** Derek gave a word that he felt CAP was a new bowl for cities, and that there would be a source of fresh water that remained pure as CAP went out.

18th October 1998

Matthew 16:18–19

> **Brian Del Turco** Says that the Lord will give us a few of the many

keys to the kingdom of heaven, and that nothing will be allowed to overcome us.

22nd October 1998

1 Samuel 2:6–10

> **Steven Spencer** At a time of persecution. A close family member launched another amazing attack, a large Trust opened up with an appalling letter saying I was basically not honourable and I was running "a business not a charity" and it was for my own benefit. The word speaks of God silencing them, and that it is God who gives strength to the ones He anoints. See Nehemiah 6:3–4

October 1998

Deuteronomy 8:17–18

> **Personal reflection** See 21st December 1996 and again here, the word says it's God who has given the ability to create wealth.

October 1998

Psalm 91 (The whole Psalm)

> **Personal reflection** An amazing psalm speaks about God's protection.

October 1998

Ecclesiastes 11:1–6

> **Personal reflection** Saying we should ask for help and let God make it happen.

October 1998

Malachi 3:6–12

> **CAP prayer team** We will be blessed because we give to God.

February 1999

Psalm 118:21–24

> **Whilst at Kings Park** Says CAP is God's capstone and that it's the Lord who has made it like it is.

May 1999

John 11:6

Personal reflection Jesus stayed a couple of extra days. This spoke to me that Jesus was not in a hurry, He knew He would get to where He wanted to get, and there was ample time. Helped me understand the times when things just didn't move forward as fast I wanted. We would get there in the end anyway!!

24th June 1999

1 Kings 17:7– 24

Paul Hubbard Word for "client giving" and Gods miraculous provision for CAP. Widow gives to a man of God before she was due to die. Give first to the man of God, through obedience and response will come provision. We are not to be afraid v13. Also Elijah had been fed by ravens God could supply his needs but sometimes God wanted others to be released form their certain death by giving. It spoke of different seasons and ways of provision. Almost an ongoing word and revelation to new staff, partner churches etc.

June 1999

Nehemiah The whole Book

Personal reflection This has been a major teaching and representation of the whole CAP journey. So much has come from this book, it's too much to write down.

June 1999

Ongoing Chapter 1 Moved by compassion to do something, prayer and asking for favour, and then starting.

June 1999

Ongoing Chapter 2 Inspecting, planning, being strategic and not telling everybody. Then rallying call v17–18 people respond and immediate opposition.

June 1999

Ongoing Chapter 3 speaks of each person doing their bit, major part of CAP's plan, a body all working towards one goal.

June 1999

> **Ongoing** Chapter 4 More opposition, half built. Ridicule and threats. Jews themselves speak against the work. Change in strategy, stationing guards and reminding people God is with them. v16 protecting what was already achieved. Year of consolidation 2002–03 and throughout the whole of CAP.

June 1999

> **Ongoing** Chapter 5 Helps the poor, puts God's laws and fairness into action.

June 1999

> **Ongoing** Chapter 6, 21 Oct 1998 great personal attack from close family member and large Trust. Nehemiah knows he's right and just gets on with it. The wall is rebuilt.

June 1999

> **Ongoing** Chapter 7 all about people returning to Jerusalem. Speaks of the evangelistic work of CAP, new homes, new families.

June 1999

> **Ongoing** Chapter 8 Ezra read the law. Speaks that God's word is to be why we do what we do. Nehemiah was happy to let others bring spiritual wisdom and teaching. We have been blessed with such people like Paul Hubbard (initial Chairman and now Trustee), and Debbie Thompson (National Prayer co–ordinator) here at CAP.

June 1999

> **Ongoing** Chapter 9 Repentance, turning back to God. This is what CAP is. The rest of the book is about order discipline and appointing people, but also keeping the whole thing pure. A continual process within CAP.

June 1999

> *2 Kings 7:1–19*
>
> **Personal reflection** As a ministry we are almost in a permanent state of nowhere to go, but to go forward, it somehow does not get any easier. This word is about four lepers with nowhere to go, but God

went before them as they stepped out and performed a miracle. This word also speaks of the officer who spoke out and doubted the man of God and his faith, he actually missed the whole miracle. We know many have spoken out their lack of faith in how we operate, despite the miraculous intervention of God at every turn.

September 1999

Joshua 14:6–15

Caleb given Hebron. Speaks of following God wholeheartedly with conviction, asking God for the mountain. Go out and battle, just get stuck in.

8th November 1999

Psalm 102:2–11

Personal reflection Desperate time of real pressure, just crying out to God to come quick.

November 1999

Ecclesiastes 11:1–6

Personal reflection At a time when it looked very difficult, felt the Lord say, "Just press on. Even though it looks doomed it's not, and you will reap a harvest".

4th February 2000

1 Samuel 14:1–23

Rob Garratt Speaks of God's miraculous intervention, Rob said just hold on, keep going.

June 2000

2 Corinthians 8:1–15

Josie Barlow (CAP Funding and P.R. Manager) About the grace of giving and how important God thinks it is. He puts it alongside love v7. This has been a great encourager to us all, in realising giving is an act of worship; and by encouraging people to give, God is getting all the glory and the worship.

July 2000

2 Corinthians 9:6 –15

Josie Barlow (CAP Funding and P.R. Manager) About giving and God wanting us to be cheerful givers.

23rd October 2000

Jeremiah 32:9–15

Personal reflection On the verge of buying what was to become "Jubilee Mill". This was confirmation that I should press ahead and try and buy the Mill irrespective of what it looked like.

23rd October 2000

Jeremiah 32:43–44

Personal reflection This was the crucial day that I made the offer for "Jubilee Mill". Felt the Lord confirming it would all work out and it would not be the last piece of land we were to get. (We now have three pieces of land in the area).

23rd October 2000

Jeremiah 33:9–12

Personal reflection As we bought the Mill, felt the Lord saying he would honour us and we would effect the area around the Mill.

8th November 2000

Psalm 27:1–5

Lesley Shepherd Just as we were about to start buying Jubilee Mill, speaks of God's power and confirmation.

7th February 2001

Joshua 5:13–15

Personal reflection (whilst skiing in Tignes) The fall of Jericho. Joshua gave up: 1) his self-will to the Lord; 2) surrendered his self effort, (God will do it not you); 3) self glory. It's God's glory not yours. This is how we aim to be with CAP, it's a "God thing".

29th April 2001

Proverbs 8

Paul Hubbard Very important Proverb for CAP, speaks of God's wisdom speaking out, and of how vital it is we get His wisdom. Says that at cross roads His wisdom shouts, it's loud. We have continually increased our "shouting" to clients, that the CAP way is the right way out of debt and poverty.

29th April 2001
Luke 2:52

> **Paul Hubbard** Paul felt that I would grow in stature in both the sight of God and Man, and that I needed to be aware of the possibility that pride might raise itself up. (Good word).

19th June 2001
Joel 2:29–32

> **Tim Griffiths** It says that God will perform wonders here on earth, and that salvation is the answer, and that all who call on him shall be saved.

21st June 2001
Lamentations 3:23–24

> **Personal reflection** Speaks of how great the Lord's faithfulness is, and that I just have to wait on him.

24th June 2001
Psalm 84:5–7

> **Personal reflection** The strength we have is from God not of our own making. We are doing something, going somewhere and in the process becoming more like Jesus. Praise God!!

June 2001
Ephesians 2:20–22

> **Paul Hubbard** About us all working together, with different gifts, which are all gifts from God and need to be honoured.

25th July 2001
Psalm 91

> **Personal reflection** That no harm will come to those who draw near to God.

26th July 2001

Proverbs 3:3–18

> **Personal reflection** Amazing, and one of my favourite Proverbs. Speaks of Gods promises, direction and wisdom.

26th July 2001

2 Kings 7:1–19

> **Personal reflection** Many times over the years. 1st was 26th July 2001, needed £70,000 to get up to date, as we have many times since, we had absolutely nowhere to go, we could not go back, we had no alternative but to go forward. As the Lord did with these four lepers, He has always gone before us, and many miracles have been performed.

27th July 2001

Psalm 102:2–11

> **Personal reflection** End of fifth year. Still huge financial problems, two months behind, still crying out to God.

29th July 2001

Isaiah 11:2–5

> **Steve Sheldon** Steve felt that this is how we are and will be with the poor and needy, that we will have Jesus' heart towards the poor!!

July 2001

Luke 14:15–23

> **Matt Barlow** The parable of the great banquet, how we should invite the poor into our houses.

July 2001

1 Kings 10:6–15

> **John Mitchell** Speaks of God's provision for me personally.

July 2001

Proverbs 28:8

> **Personal reflection** Just as we began to ask the finance industry for funding and support.

July 2001

Isaiah 30:21

> **Personal reflection** Says there is voice behind you which says "This is the way; walk in it" I have received this word at many times of great need and much opposition.

July 2001

Isaiah 58:9–12

> **Personal reflection** Wonderful word of encouragement.

July 2001

Jeremiah 17:7–8

> **Personal reflection** Says that blessed is the man who trusts in the lord, he will be fruitful. This was at a time of pressure and stress.

19th August 2001

Matthew 21:13

> **Personal reflection** Spoke of the need for an increase of prayer for the charity and in my own life. Debbie Thompson began to make sure prayer was more established within the charity. Within the year she was employed as National Prayer Co–ordinator, now co–ordinating prayer in 29 centres.

19th August 2001

1 Peter 2:4–6

> **Paul Hubbard** This says that we are to be spiritual yet practical.

2nd September 2001

Colossians 3:1–4

> **Paul Hubbard** It's about setting our hearts on things above, not on earthly things. Always good when things look bad and you are in need.

2nd September 2001

Matthew 3:13–17

> **Paul Hubbard** Says that we need to repent and be baptised, that we can easily get our lives in order.

2nd September 2001

Ephesians 3:14–21

Personal reflection This speaks of God's amazing power to do abundantly more than we ask or imagine. This has become a major force in our faith, that God is able to do more than we can think, and it spurs us on to greater hopes for the future.

14th September 2001

Isaiah 55:2–5

Personal reflection The Lord saying He would continue to fill the empty jars we brought to Him, but we must not stop bringing the empty jars as that could stop his flow!!

5th November 2001

Hebrews 10:32–39

Clive Boldy Speaks of remembering how hard it has been, and the way we were when it all started, and to press on as God is coming quick.

December 2001

1 Chronicles 4:9–10

Gary Jones Gary Jones got saved and gave me this wonderful book by Bruce Wilkinson *Prayer of Jabez*. We basically continually pray this prayer, and believe that God will bless us in all we do, enlarge our territory, be with us and protect us from harm.

February 2002

2 Samuel 6:14, 21–23

Derek Brown Speaks of total focus on the Lord, and that some will speak against what I do, but they will be sorted out by God not me.

February 2002

Psalm 67: 1–7

Derek Brown Speaks of the effect of praise and worship in breaking through (how true).

February 2002

Proverbs 8

> **Personal reflection** CAP conference "Wisdom Shouts".

February 2002

Ezekiel 47: 1–12

> **Personal reflection** Speaks of being in deep water and having no option but to swim. I feel totally out of my depth, and almost resigned to swimming or sinking.

February 2002

James 1: 2–13

> **Personal reflection** "Consider it pure joy when you face trials of many kinds . . ." This has been a source of constant encouragement over the years, to press through the huge difficulties we have faced.

15th March 2002

Habakkuk 3: 17–19

> **Steven Roberts** Need £105,000 in 6 weeks. This word says that I will rejoice in the Lord and He will get us through,

2nd April 2002

Psalm 37: 1–7

> **Personal reflection** The day a close friend said: no support and you are making a huge mistake. We need £80,000 today!! All looks lost after six years hard graft. Still where I was six years ago, totally reliant on God. (By 14th June all wages paid!!).

2nd April 2002

Psalm 37:19

> **Personal reflection** Says in times of disaster they will not wither; in days of famine they will enjoy plenty.

2nd April 2002

Psalm 40:1–4

> **Personal reflection** Black Tuesday, says God will turn up and that we are blessed, because we make the Lord our trust.

2nd April 2002

Psalm 40:11–12

> **Personal reflection** Asking God for mercy.

2nd April 2002

Psalm 40:13–17

> **Personal reflection** Pleading for God to turn up quickly!

2nd April 2002

Psalm 41:1

> **Personal reflection** Say the Lord delivers him in times of trouble.

2nd April 2002

Psalm 41

> **Personal reflection** Very difficult time. This Psalm speaks of God upholding us. Speaks of feeling abandoned by some.

2nd April 2002

Proverbs 3:25

> **Personal reflection** Says "Have no fear of sudden disaster." This is a very difficult time.

2nd April 2002

Isaiah 51:7–8

> **Personal reflection** Very difficult time, felt the Lord saying I did not need to fear what man thought, and that he would get us through.

2nd April 2002

Isaiah 58:9–12

> **Personal reflection** Very difficult time, but felt God return me to the word he gave me all those years ago.

2nd April 2002

Isaiah 55:8–9

> **Personal reflection** Says that his thoughts are not our thoughts and his ways are higher than our ways. Praise God, he knows what he's doing, sometimes I have absolutely no idea!!

2nd April 2002

Hebrews 10:32–39

Clive Boldy This word really encouraged me just to press forward as I have done over the years, despite great difficulties at the time.

2nd April 2002

Exodus 33:12–21

Needed £88,000 today and £109,000 in nine weeks. Very difficult time, just been told it would all fall apart if I didn't change how we operated. Reassurance that God is with us. An exaltation that God is with Moses. v21 says there is a place near Jesus that you may stand on a rock.

2nd April 2002

Joshua 1:5–9

Black Tuesday, the day someone said no support, and you are making huge mistake. Need £80,000 today!! All looks lost after six years hard graft still where I was six years ago totally reliant on God. (By 14th June all wages paid!!)

4th April 2002

Matthew 27:45–53

From Ray Bevan's teachings This is the death of Jesus. Ray said that it's not how you are when things are great, it's how you are when you feel like you are helpless and totally reliant on God. It's then that the resurrection power of God is released.

10th April 2002

Psalm 142:3–6

From Ray Bevan's teachings Basically says that God is still here even when you can't see him or feel him.

10th April 2002

Isaiah 43:1–3

From Ray Bevan's teachings A great word of encouragement saying God will get me through. Ray said that we had to go "through" some things to get an understanding and a maturity in God that could not be received in any other way.

11th April 2002

Acts 27:23–44

> **From Ray Bevan's teachings** The shipwreck of Paul. A time of great difficulties and pressure, felt the Lord encouraging me that we would get through whatever it looked like.

12th April 2002

Psalm 27:13–14

> **Personal reflection** Very difficult time. Our faith to carry on was being severely tested. Says be strong and take heart.

13th April 2002

Luke 16:19–31

> **Personal reflection** A great call to evangelism.

16th April 2002

Numbers 11:1–5

> **Nick Clarke** Hard times, speaks of not grumbling.

22nd April 2002

Isaiah 58:9–12

> **Personal reflection** Whilst in Australia. Speaking of the same anointing that we have in the UK, to break the yoke of oppression.

April 2002

Isaiah 55:4–5

> **Personal reflection** Whilst in Australia. For the first time felt the Lord confirm that nations would come to us to find out the secrets he had given us. Huge word but very encouraging to actually see people in other nations listening to us and starting to duplicate the work of CAP.

April 2002

Psalm 102:17–18

> **Personal reflection** Says God will respond to the prayer of the destitute and will not despise their plea. We need Him to turn up very soon.

April 2002

Isaiah 42:1–4

> **Personal reflection** Whilst in Australia. Seeing CAP Oz begin to take off. Felt the Lord saying to me that we should not falter or be discouraged, but should press on.

13th May 2002

Joshua 5:11–12

> Very stressed time. No money, two months down with wages. The word speaks of God's promise that we will eat. Says that there is a change coming in that we will eat from the land and not direct manna as we have in the past!!

18th May 2002

Numbers 20:9–12

> **Debbie Thompson** Very hard times. Possibly asking for staff to miss one month's wage. Word speaks of Moses striking the rock when the Lord had said speak to it. Debbie felt it was like taking things into our own hands and not trusting God. (By 14th June up to date with wages and all staff paid). Debbie felt we should not lose faith now!! How right she was!! (See Deuteronomy 32:51–52).

18th May 2002

Deuteronomy 32:51–52

> See Numbers 20:9–11 This word speaks at the consequences of losing faith and taking things into your own hands Very testing time at CAP.

22nd May 2002

Deuteronomy 11:8–16, 22–25

> **Personal reflection** Six years on still need £45,000 for this year, and we have shortfall of £404,000 for next year. Speaks of a land we are about to enter which is fed by waters from heaven, and that in the past we have had to work very hard for each drop of water, from now on it will flow down hill with gravity. A promise of taking nations and God will give us success.

May 2002

Ezra 4:1–5

Personal reflection Speaks of opposition. At the time closing a centre who wanted to do things their way and not embrace CAP.

22nd June 2002

Jonah 1:4–5

From Ray Bevan's teachings Speaks of how rough it gets when you get out of God's will, and that God will work all things for the good of everybody who follows after him.

25th June 2002

Isaiah 46:4

Personal reflection My Mother had a cancer and needed an operation and radiotherapy. God said she would be healed, and she was. Praise God!!

3rd July 2002

Ezekiel 36:9–11

Alan Siderfin Speaks of God's abundant provision and massive increase in our fruitfulness.

July 2002

I Corinthians 12:12–26

Personal reflection This speaks of the one body many parts within CAP, and that we are all working together in unity for one aim.

July 2002

Genesis 39:3, 21

It's about God being with us all. The Lord was with Joseph and He is with me.

July 2002

Isaiah 61:1–4

Personal reflection Always a source of great encouragement to us all. Got a sense that we have been involved in creating a massive number of "Oaks of righteousness, a planting of the Lord for the display of His splendour" as 100's have come to know the Lord through the work.

July 2002

Luke 12:16–19

> **Keith Tondeur** The rich man and his barns. The lord showed us that its not about "I" or "me" it's about others.

July 2002

Romans 12:3

> **Paul Hubbard** About having a sober judgement of your ability. This is a great word for every Christian.

3rd August 2002

Psalm 23:1–6

> **Rose Mitchell** Rose said she felt the Lord say we should just lie down with Him.

5th August 2002

Psalm 91

> **John Mitchell** Great word of the Lord's heart towards me, and that he would never let me go, and that everything is under control.

5th August 2002

John 12:25–26

> **John Mitchell** Spoke of God honouring us as we serve him.

11th August 2002

Proverbs 24:30–34

> **From Paul Scanlon's teaching** Speaks how little things can have a great effect on our circumstances. Says how simple Jesus was in his explanations because he came for the poor, needy and simple at heart.

August 2002

Ecclesiastes 9:4

> **From Ramson Mumba's teaching** Says even a live dog is better than a dead Lion. i.e. where there is breath there is hope!! This is a great word when things look bleak, we have never stopped, therefore there has always been life and hope. It's when you stop that you are in trouble.

August 2002

Matthew 11:28–30

Personal reflection The Lord showed me how CAP mirrors this passage in showing people God's rest for the weary. I have preached with this to encourage evangelism, God has blessed it.

August 2002

Mark 6:3–4

Personal reflection Speaks of people who know you easily take offence. That you can be easily and unfairly rejected, particularly in your own town.

August 2002

Mark 6:47–52

Paul Hubbard This is where Jesus is in the boat and a wind came against them, and how Jesus calmed the storm. I felt it was the Lord saying a strong contra wind had come up against us, but Jesus was in the boat and we needed faith that the boat would not be overwhelmed.

August 2002

1 Peter 4:12–16

Personal reflection Speaks about suffering and not to be surprised when we faced painful trials. Very encouraging at all times of difficulties.

11th September 2002

Isaiah 45:3

Personal reflection Been going exactly six years from first client in Sep 1996. Need £80,000 to get up to date, and can't quite believe we are *still* struggling as much as we are.

September 2002

Isaiah 54:2–7

Personal reflection Can't pay salaries, bills etc. Feel as if I am totally disgraced and humiliated. Felt the lord say that we are not disgraced or humiliated in *his* eyes, and that he delights in our faith and resolve against massive difficulties. We need £80,000 to pay back wages and bills!!

1st October 2002

Psalm 23:1–6

> **Personal reflection** Whilst in London speaking at St Marks, Battersea.

October 2002

John 4:6

> **Personal reflection** Says Jesus was tired but still managed to minister to the women at the well. This spoke of the fact that it was OK to be tired but always be open to an opportunity to minister.

8th December 2002

John 14:26

> **From Paul Scanlon's teachings** About the Holy Spirit being our guide and how important it is we stay in the "bulls eye" of God's purpose for us, when we find it. I felt the Lord say that CAP was my "bulls eye".